GUIDE TO BEER

GUIDE TO BEER

ROBERT JACKSON AND DAVID KENNING

Parragon

Bath · New York · Singapore · Hong Kong · Cologne · Delhi · Melbourne

First published by Parragon in 2008

Parragon
Queen Street House
4 Queen Street
Bath BA1 1HE, UK

ISBN: 978-1-4075-1773-5

Editorial and design by
Amber Books Ltd
Bradley's Close
74–77 White Lion Street
London N1 9PF
United Kingdom
www.amberbooks.co.uk

Project Editor: James Bennett
Design: Tony Cohen
Picture Research: Kate Green

Printed in China

CONTENTS

Introduction

'Beer is proof that God loves us and wants us to be happy' – Benjamin Franklin

It is hard to say for sure when, exactly, the first true beers were brewed, but it is likely that they originated in the Middle East and Egypt. The first detailed reports of brewing as we understand it were recorded more than 5,000 years ago by the Sumerians, who lived in the land between the Rivers Tigris and Euphrates, which roughly equates to modern-day Iraq. After the Sumerians, the ancient Egyptians developed the art of brewing on a large scale to supply the pharaoh's armies with a daily ration, and also refined the process of malting.

Countless variations on the basic recipe for beer exist, using all manner of ingredients. Some of these added ingredients are considered 'adjuncts', used as a cheap alternative for malted barley, predominantly in mass-produced industrial lagers. Common examples are sugar, rice, maize, corn syrup and malt extracts. However, other grains like wheat and oats have a more legitimate claim for use in traditional beer styles, and some other ingredients can be considered genuine flavour enhancers. These might be blends of herbs and spices, such as juniper, coriander, ginger, and orange and lemon peel. The tradition of using honey to flavour beer stretches back centuries, while in Scotland, heather is used by one brewery to flavour its beer.

Although the basic brewing process is much the same for every beer, the endless variations in proportions of ingredients, types of water, malts, yeast and hops, not to mention the various other ingredients used, plus the different conditions under which each beer is brewed, give rise to a highly diverse and varied product. The positive side to this is that you need not be restricted to calling a single beer your favourite. The truth is that there is a different beer for every occasion, whether it be a simple refreshing thirst-quencher on a hot summer's day, or a strong, dark beer to serve with a celebratory meal in winter.

Left: Belgian Lambic beer is brewed using only wild yeasts grown from airborne spores. The result is a highly unusual beer which is dry, vinous, and cidery, with a slightly sour aftertaste.

Right: One of Germany's most famous beer exports, Beck's is a popular pilsener-style lager with a crisp, clean taste. As well as at its birthplace in Bremen, Germany, Beck's is also brewed in Australia, Bulgaria, China, Montenegro, Nigeria, Romania, Serbia, Turkey and Ukraine.

MOLSON
CANADIAN

Canadian Beers

Taxes on alcohol are among the highest in the world in this country, making beer in Canada expensive, and local laws prevent the selling of beer across provincial boundaries. As a result of both of these factors, beer production in Canada has traditionally been dominated by a handful of large brewing groups.

Molson, the largest, was founded in Montreal in 1786 by Englishman John Molson. The next largest, Carling, was established in Ontario by Sir Thomas Carling in 1840 and merged with local rival O'Keefe in 1862 to form Carling O'Keefe, which was ultimately taken over by Molson in 1989. The other major Canadian player, Labatt, was founded by Irishman John Labatt in 1847. Foreign interests now own Labatt and Molson. Labatt has been part of Belgian conglomerate Interbrew since 1995, and in 2004 Molson merged with giant US brewer Coors.

These big, powerful companies are able to circumvent the local laws by opening regional brewing plants across the country, often by swallowing up smaller local brands. On a more positive note, the restrictions have also enabled many small microbreweries to spring up, content to operate within provincial boundaries and produce interesting craft beers on a small scale, though the market is still dominated by light, bland lagers. In spite of draconian licensing laws, Canadian brewers have always led the way in advancing brewing technology. Labatt, in particular, introduced its Ice beer, in 1993.

Left: Molson is one of the world's largest brewers, with operations in Canada, Brazil and the United States. Molson Canadian lager, a crisp, easy-drinking beer, is very popular. Other beers in the Molson Canadian family include Molson Canadian Ice, Canada's best-selling ice beer. Molson traces its roots back to 1786, making it North America's oldest beer brand.

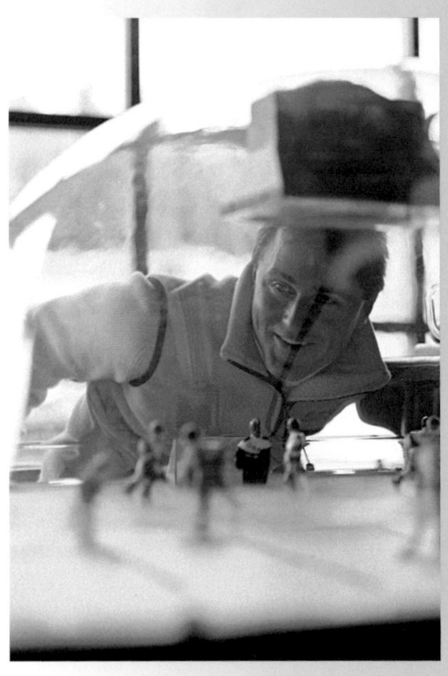

Above: Canadian cities have a thriving pub and bar culture, providing a ready and enthusiastic market for local microbreweries.

STATISTICS

Total production: 23,443,000 hectolitres (619,299,000 gallons) per year

Consumption per capita: 60 litres (16 gallons) per year

Famous breweries: Big Rock; Creemore Springs; Labatt; McAuslan; Molson; Moosehead; Unibroue

Famous brands: Creemore Springs Premium Lager; Grasshöpper; Labatt Ice Beer; Moosehead Lager; Molson Canadian

Alexander Keith's IPA

Brewed in Halifax, Nova Scotia, Alexander Keith's India Pale Ale originated in 1820, when the brewery owner decided to produce quality beers and ales that could be enjoyed across a wide cross-section of the community.

This particular India pale ale is a clear, light yellow ale with a small but distinctly fizzy head. The flavour is a pleasant combination of tangy and sweet, and there are additional hints of apricot, honey and butterscotch. The ale also gives an excellent, nutty aftertaste, and in general is greatly refreshing. Some critics, however, suggest that Alexander Keith's IPA is not a traditional India pale ale because it is not malty enough. Others also recommend the drink more as a draught rather than a bottled product. Whatever the varying opinions may be, the IPA certainly has a solid following.

SPECIFICATIONS

Brewery: Alexander Keith's (Labatt/Inbev)
Location: Halifax, Novia Scotia
Style: India pale ale
Colour: Light yellow
Alcohol: 5%
Serving temperature: 5°–7°C (41°–44.6°F)
Food: Bread with mature Cheddar cheese

Grasshöpper

A unique wheat ale that is easy to drink and exceptionally refreshing, Grasshöpper is delicately hopped and delivers a smooth, bright finish.

Grasshöpper is influenced by Germany's Kristall Weisen and is one of several popular products of the Big Rock Brewery, founded in the mid-1980s by Ed McNally, a Canadian of Irish descent. McNally originally trained as a lawyer, but abandoned that trade to become first a farmer, then a beverage entrepreneur. Grasshöpper is a clear ale with a slightly lemony aroma, and is crisp and sharp on the palate. The ale, which has a sunny ambient yellow colour, retains its head for quite some time after pouring.

SPECIFICATIONS

Brewery: Big Rock
Location: Calgary, Alberta
Style: Wheat ale
Colour: Golden-yellow
Alcohol: 5%
Serving temperature: 5°C (41°F)
Food: Any spicy oriental dish

Creemore Springs Premium Lager

Available in both bottled and draught form, Creemore Springs Premium Lager has a good balance of hops with a touch of honey in the malt. It has a pleasant, homely quality with a slight citrus aroma and a fresh, crisp taste reminiscent of a good pilsener.

The brew is sweet, but not overwhelmingly so. Golden orange when poured, it has a small head that soon disappears to leave a pleasing lacy effect. The brewery, located in the village of Creemore, has the advantage of access to pure spring water bubbled through a limestone bed and used in the brewing process. Creemore publicity emphasizes that the 'unique amber lager is fire brewed in small batches and delivered fresh weekly'. Devotees of Creemore beers can belong to an official fan club run by the brewery.

SPECIFICATIONS

Brewery: Creemore Springs
Location: Creemore, Ontario
Style: Premium lager
Colour: Golden orange
Alcohol: 5%
Serving temperature: 5°C (41°F)
Food: Beef or pork

Labatt Ice

When it was introduced in 1993, Labatt Ice was the world's first ice beer. It is created using a unique process in which the beer is chilled to around -4°C, at which temperature ice crystals begin to form.

These ice crystals are then removed, leaving a smoother, lighter beer; as water freezes at a higher temperature than alcohol, the proportion of alcohol in the beer also increases. Extra smoothness is achieved through lengthy maturation, and selected North American and European hops are used to create a full yet delicate flavour. Today the Labatt 'family' of brands incorporates a wide range of styles.

SPECIFICATIONS

Brewery: Labatt
Location: Toronto, Ontario
Style: Ice beer
Colour: Pale golden yellow
Alcohol: 5.6%
Serving temperature: 6°C (42.8°F)
Food: Spicy chicken dishes

Griffon Extra Blonde

In 1989, Montreal man Peter McAuslan, believing that he could brew a beer better than any of the others that were available locally, set up the McAuslan brewery.

His products fall into two groups, each with its own branding: St-Ambroise and Griffon. The two Griffon beers are the Irish-style red ale, made with roasted barley and crystal malt for a nutty, malty flavour, and Extra Pale Ale, a golden ale with a well-balanced hop and malt flavour. Both have won several awards, including a gold medal at the 1996 World Beer Cup for Extra Pale Ale. McAuslan Griffon is keen to promote cooking with its beers, and recommends using its products in recipes including soda bread, carrot and sweet potato soup, apricot chicken pilaf with almonds, and chocolate stout mousse.

SPECIFICATIONS
Brewery: McAuslan
Location: Montreal, Quebec
Style: Pale ale
Colour: Golden yellow
Alcohol: 5%
Serving temperature: 8°–10°C (46.4°–50°F)
Food: A hearty vegetable soup

St-Ambroise Oatmeal Stout

Among the many awards to come the way of Montreal's McAuslan brewery has been a Platinum Medal for its St-Ambroise Oatmeal Stout at the 1994 World Beer Championship, along with the second-highest rating of more than 200 beers.

A high proportion of dark malts and roasted barley give this rich black ale a powerful aroma that is redolent of coffee and chocolate, while the oatmeal produces a remarkably smooth and full-bodied texture. A light balancing hop bitterness, with a hint of grass in the aroma and a crisp, dry finish, makes this a very well rounded beer and surprisingly light and easy drinking.

SPECIFICATIONS
Brewery: McAuslan
Location: Montreal, Quebec
Style: Oatmeal stout
Colour: Deep opaque black
Alcohol: 5%
Serving temperature: 12°C (53.6°F)
Food: Rich chocolate cake

Molson Canadian

Molson, North America's oldest brewery, produces this classic lager using only the finest hops, crystal-clear water and malted barley.

Established in 1786 by John Molson, who founded a brewery on the St Lawrence River near Montreal, Quebec, Molson produces a great many popular brews. Indeed, Molson himself commented in 1786 on his beer's popularity, saying: 'My beer has been universally well liked beyond my most sanguine expectations.' The same seems to hold true today. One of its best-selling brands, this lager is smooth, with a hint of bitterness. Each brew is fermented slowly to produce its characteristic taste. Molson Canadian is an 'easy' drink, very popular at parties, and should never be served warm. Served cold, its taste is crisp, modern and extremely refreshing.

SPECIFICATIONS
Brewery: Molson
Location: Toronto, Ontario
Style: Lager
Colour: Golden yellow
Alcohol: 5%
Serving temperature: 5°–7°C (41°–44.6°F)
Food: Cold chicken salad

Rickard's Red

Rickard's Red, another offering from Molson, has remained Canada's top-selling red beer for more than 10 years.

First brewed in Vancouver at the original site of the Capilano brewery in the early 1980s, Rickard's Red is made with a unique blend of three different malted barleys. The result is an unbelievably smooth and delicious red beer with exceptional drinkability. A very well balanced drink, creamy and malty, it has just the right amount of flavour and carbonation. Rickard's Red occupies the mid range of alcohol content in the Molson brands. At the bottom are beers such as Molson Ultra (4.5%), while climbing above Rickard's Red are Molson Dry (5.5%) and the potent alcomalt Tornade (6.0%).

SPECIFICATIONS
Brewery: Molson
Location: Toronto, Ontario
Style: Dark ale
Colour: Reddish-brown
Alcohol: 5.2%
Serving temperature: 5.6°C (42°F)
Food: Roast beef or pork salad

Moosehead Lager

The history of Moosehead Breweries, now located in Saint John, New Brunswick, began in 1867, when Susannah Oland first brewed a solitary batch of brown October ale in her backyard in neighbouring Nova Scotia.

Encouraged by friends and family, Susannah and her husband, John James Dunn Oland, began to market the beer. Since then, the firm has survived a succession of disasters, including the explosion that wrecked Halifax in 1917, to produce one of the finest premium lagers in North America. A smooth, clean-tasting lager well balanced between malt sweetness and hop bitterness, it is brewed from a blend of Canadian Barley malt, two types of hops, and fresh water from nearby Spruce Lake. The lager is then aged a full 28 days.

SPECIFICATIONS
Brewery: Moosehead
Location: Saint John, New Brunswick
Style: Classic American lager
Colour: Golden yellow
Alcohol: 5%
Serving temperature: 5°C (41°F)
Food: Curries

Blanche de Chambly

A product of the successful Unibroue, Blanche de Chambly is a naturally cloudy, unfiltered Belgian-style golden wheat beer.

Its aroma and flavour are redolent with zesty orange and lemon and light fruity malts, backed up by hints of coriander, ginger and other spices. The high carbonation gives the beer a Champagne-like appearance and a spritzy mouthfeel, while light hopping provides a refreshingly dry finish. It is no coincidence that the brewery's products have a Franco-Belgian character; the company was founded in 1991 by Belgian beer enthusiast André Dion, with guidance through its early stages from the highly regarded Liefmans and Riva breweries of Belgium.

SPECIFICATIONS
Brewery: Unibroue
Location: Chambly, Quebec
Style: Witbier / Belgian wheat beer
Colour: Pale golden
Alcohol: 5%
Serving temperature: 8°–10°C (46.4°–50°F)
Food: Poultry, fish and shellfish

La Fin du Monde

Unibroue has a large range of characterful bottle-conditioned beers. Its La Fin du Monde (French for 'the end of the world') is inspired by the Belgian triple ales produced by the Trappist monks.

Traditionally, these rich, spicy ales were brewed to drink on special occasions. This example – made with pale Pilsener malt and imported German and Belgian hops – has a typically powerful aroma of spicy hops balanced by rich fruity malt and citrus notes. On the palate, hops and malt vie for attention, but the flavour is well balanced and surprisingly subtle, enhanced with wild spices. La Fin du Monde has a smooth, creamy body and a long finish that becomes increasingly dry and bitter.

SPECIFICATIONS
Brewery: Unibroue
Location: Chambly, Quebec
Style: Belgian abbey triple
Colour: Deep golden yellow
Alcohol: 9%
Serving temperature: 14°C (57.2°F)
Food: Fine cheeses and desserts

Wellington Iron Duke

Wellington Iron Duke is an English-style strong ale, a product of Wellington County Brewery in Ontario.

Dark ruby colour with a fully diminishing fizzy and frothy tan head, it has a dark fruit, toffee and cherry aroma, as well as dark fruit, plum, raisin, light toffee and alcohol flavours. The ale is full-bodied, with a dry and lightly fizzy mouthfeel. The small head has a rather nutty taste, and the aftertaste is malty and mellow. From the start, Wellington County used North American raw materials, but also British malts and traditional English hop varieties. The brewery's strong ale is named after the Duke of Wellington, who defeated Napoleon at Waterloo.

SPECIFICATIONS
Brewery: Wellington County
Location: Guelph, Ontario
Style: English strong ale
Colour: Dark ruby
Alcohol: 6.5%
Serving temperature: 6°C (42.8°F)
Food: Roast beef, steak and kidney pudding, mature Cheddar

THOMAS KEMPER
IRON TUB
PORTER
NOT PERMITTED
Pyramid
SEATTLE • BERKELEY

American Beers

The United States is the world's largest brewing nation. The story of how it arrived at this position begins in 1612, with the establishment of the first brewery by early colonial settlers. Waves of immigrants from Britain, Ireland, the Netherlands and Germany all brought a love of beer with them and set up numerous breweries.

The importance of beer in the history of the United States cannot be overstated. Several key American historical figures were brewers, including George Washington and Thomas Jefferson, and British taxation imposed on colonial breweries was one of the triggers for the Revolution.

The puritanical temperance movement's efforts led to prohibition in several states in the 1850s, although this ended with the American Civil War. During World War I, prohibitionists argued that alcohol production should be banned to conserve grain. By 1919, prohibition was national, ruining most of the breweries and forcing liquor production underground. In 1933 Franklin Roosevelt was elected President on the strength of a pledge to repeal Prohibition.

After the end of Prohibition, brewing came to be dominated by a small handful of long-established breweries. Names such as Anheuser-Busch (Budweiser) and Miller gained a dominance that they hold to this day, their beers accounting for around 80% of all domestic sales. Since the late 1970s, however, a new generation of enthusiasts has begun to re-establish small-scale craft brewing. Some of these new brews hark back to the traditional European beer styles brewed by their ancestors, while others are the result of a more innovative approach, producing full-flavoured modern beers characterized by exciting use of new hops varieties. The industry now flourishes, with well over 1000 microbreweries, ranging from tiny brewpubs to larger concerns such as Sierra Nevada in California, with the capacity to distribute their beers across the nation.

Left: A new generation of craft brewers has also given a new lease of life to the traditional pub. Establishments such as this, in Seattle, Washington, now stock a huge range of flavoursome and unusual beers, both home-brewed and imported.

Above: Notable US microbreweries featured in this book include BridgePort of Portland, Oregon; Michigan Brewing Company of Webberville, Michigan; and New Glarus Brewing Company of Wisconsin.

STATISTICS

Total production: 232,216,000 hectolitres (6,134,498,000 gallons) per year

Consumption per capita: 84 litres (22 gallons) per year

Famous breweries: Anheuser-Busch; Brooklyn; Coors; Latrobe; SAB Miller; Sierra Nevada

Famous brands: Bud Lite; Busch; Celis White; Coors Original; Michelob; Miller Genuine Draft; Miller Lite; Pabst (Heileman's) Old Style; Redhook ESB; Rolling Rock

Anchor Liberty Ale

San Francisco's Anchor Brewing produces a range of seven regular and seasonal ales. One of its most popular is Liberty Ale, first brewed in 1975 to commemorate the bicentennial of Paul Revere's famous 1775 ride, marking the start of the American War of Independence.

It became a regular fixture in Anchor's repertoire in 1983. American pale ales are inspired by classic British bitters – typically a bright, clear bronze or copper colour and well flavoured with hops to give them a characteristically dry flavour. Liberty Ale is a fine example, with a rich, complex aroma redolent with floral, resiny, citric hops combined with sweet, biscuity malts. The flavour is dominated by slightly astringent hops balanced with light, fruity maltiness, and the finish is dry and refreshing with hints of lemon zest.

SPECIFICATIONS
Brewery: Anchor
Location: San Francisco, CA

Style: American pale ale
Colour: Clear amber
Alcohol: 6.1%
Serving temperature: 10°C (50°F)
Food: Steak and ale pie

Bud Light

Bud Light, a lower-calorie version of the classic Budweiser, was introduced nationally in 1982 as Budweiser Light. Since 2001, Bud Light has been the best-selling beer in the United States.

Bud Light is brewed with a malt and hops ration different from that of Budweiser to give distinctly crisp taste with only 110 calories. It makes a good, refreshing drink on a hot day, although it lacks the crispness of Budweiser. It produces a slight lacy effect and there is a gentle aroma. Some critics claim that this beer lacks flavour, but this is not so; it is pleasant to the palate and there is quite a satisfying aftertaste. All in all, this is a good picnic beer, and is best drunk straight from the can. It is definitely worth exploring.

SPECIFICATIONS
Brewery: Anheuser-Busch
Location: St Louis, MO
Style: Pale lager
Colour: Pale gold

Alcohol: 4.2%
Serving temperature: 9°–10°C (48°–50°F)
Food: Grilled chicken and salads

Busch

A typical American lager, Busch was originally known as Busch Bavarian Beer when it was introduced in the Midwestern and Southwestern states in 1955. It went national in 1979, and the brand is now a major sponsor of the NASCAR racing series.

This is a very light beer in every category. It ranges from pale yellow to slightly golden in colour, depending on the observer's eye, and has a small aroma of corn and malt. The head is white and a little fizzy. The flavour is quite mild, with a little corn coming through, and the finish abrupt. There is some bitterness, and in general the beer is smooth and light on the palate, with gentle carbonation. This is not an unpleasing beer, and like others of similar kind it is best drunk out of doors in hot weather, as an accompaniment to a picnic.

SPECIFICATIONS
Brewery: Anheuser-Busch
Location: St Louis, MO
Style: Pale lager
Colour: Pale yellow
Alcohol: 4.1%
Serving temperature: 6°–8°C (43°–46°F)
Food: Picnic foods

Michelob

Michelob was launched by Anheuser-Busch in 1896, marketed as a 'draught beer for connoisseurs', a 'premium' beer alternative to its mainstream Budweiser brand.

Like Budweiser, Michelob is named after a famous old brewing town in the former Bohemia, now part of the Czech Republic. It is brewed with a higher percentage of two-row barley malt and imported hops to create a fuller bodied beer with a mouth-filling richness. It has a light, sweet malty aroma, and the mild, grainy sweet malt flavour also dominates on the palate, backed up with a gentle hop astringency without any bitterness. The finish is crisp and refreshing. Other names in the Michelob range include a honey lager and a pale ale.

SPECIFICATIONS
Brewery: Anheuser-Busch
Location: St Louis, MO
Style: Lager
Colour: Pale straw colour
Alcohol: 5%
Serving temperature: 6°–9°C (42.8°–48.2°F)
Food: Cooked meats and sausages

BridgePort India Pale Ale

Founded in 1984 as Columbia River Brewing, BridgePort is the oldest established craft brewery in the Pacific Northwest city of Portland, Oregon. Portland, in turn, is one of the focal points of America's healthy microbrewing industry.

The BridgePort Brewing Company is housed in a former rope factory in Portland's industrial district, where it produces its range of classic beers. No fewer than five varieties of hop are used in this award-winning India Pale Ale – Cascade, Chinook, Golding, Crystal and Northwest Ultra. It is a creamy, rich and full-flavoured beer, which is naturally conditioned in a double-fermentation process in the bottle, keg or cask to give it a resiny hop aroma with grapefruit notes, a robust hoppy palate with hints of vanilla and orange fruit, and an intensely bitter hop finish.

SPECIFICATIONS
Brewery: BridgePort
Location: Portland, OR
Style: India pale ale
Colour: Pale amber gold
Alcohol: 5.5%
Serving temperature: 12°C (53.6°F)
Food: Duck in orange sauce

Brooklyn Black Chocolate Stout

Throughout the nineteenth century Brooklyn was home to a great number of breweries, many set up by German immigrants. In the 1920s, Prohibition had a devastating effect on the brewing industry, and the last remaining brewery in Brooklyn closed in 1976.

Then in 1987 former foreign correspondent Steve Hindy and former banker Tom Potter got together to establish the Brooklyn Brewery. It moved to its present site in a former steel foundry in Williamsburg in 1996, and has since been at the forefront of New York's brewing renaissance. An immensely powerful black stout, Black Chocolate Stout is the brewery's seasonal winter beer, its aromas of roasted mocha coffee, bitter chocolate and roasted malt are followed on the palate by a smooth, rich, spicy malt character with a hint of caramel sweetness and a dry, subtly bitter hop finish.

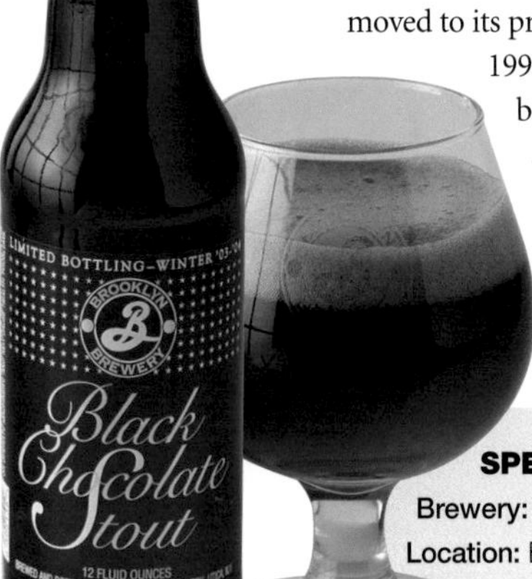

SPECIFICATIONS
Brewery: Brooklyn
Location: Brooklyn, NY
Style: Russian imperial stout
Colour: Black
Alcohol: 8.3%
Serving temperature: 13°C (55.4°F)
Food: Chocolate-based desserts

Coors Original

The Coors brewery in Golden, Colorado, is the largest single brewing site in the world. It was founded in 1873 by the 26-year-old German immigrant brewer Adolph Coors on a site chosen for the cool, clear Rocky Mountains spring water that flowed nearby.

Coors Original has a sweet malty aroma and a smooth, grainy flavour, and the beer took gold medals at the Great American Beer Festival in both 1996 and 2004. Coors Extra Gold is a full-flavoured lager brewed with lightly roasted malts. The latest addition to the range is Aspen Edge, a crisp, light-flavoured low-carbohydrate beer. Another beer in the Coors range is Blue Moon, defined by the company as 'an unfiltered wheat ale spiced in the Belgian tradition for an uncommonly smooth taste'. In 2002 Coors bought a large part of Bass from Interbrew to become the second largest brewer in the United Kingdom.

SPECIFICATIONS
Brewery: Coors
Location: Golden, CO
Style: Lager
Colour: Pale gold
Alcohol: 5%
Serving temperature: 8°C (46.4°F)
Food: Risotto and pasta

Goose Island Honkers Ale

Chicago native and beer-lover John Hall opened the Goose Island Brewery in 1998, at a time when brewpubs such as this were proliferating across America.

Goose Island's classic Honker's Ale is a subtle and elegant Pale Ale in the English style. It has a beautiful honey amber hue with a pronounced hop aroma, perfectly balancing a medium malt body and a dry hop finish. The ale pours a bright amber and is topped with a couple fingers of white frothy head. The head lingers for a couple of minutes, leaving mild lacings on the glass. The taste is hoppy, and less fruity than expected. The aftertaste is of hops and the mouthfeel is rather thin, with a smooth, creamy texture. The beer is bitter but very smooth and drinkable, leaving hops on the breath.

SPECIFICATIONS
Brewery: Goose Island
Location: Chicago, IL
Style: Pale ale
Colour: Light brown
Alcohol: 5%
Serving temperature: 10°–12°C (50°–54°F)
Food: Cold meats

Great Lakes Dortmunder Gold

This smooth, well-balanced and full-bodied lager is typical of the strong 'export' lager that became popular in Dortmund, Germany, in the mid-nineteenth century.

A Dortmunder tends to be less dry than a pilsener, but more hoppy than a pale Munich lager, and it is stronger than either. This multiple award-winning example of the style, with a deep golden colour and a grainy dry malt flavour, comes from the Great Lakes brewery and dining pub, founded in downtown Cleveland in 1988. The pub is said to have been popular in a previous incarnation with Cleveland's most famous resident, the 'untouchable' Eliot Ness.

SPECIFICATIONS
Brewery: Great Lakes
Location: Cleveland, OH
Style: Dortmunder export
Colour: Deep golden amber
Alcohol: 5.6%
Serving temperature: 9°C (48.2°F)
Food: Salads, fish and chicken

Rolling Rock

Ever since it was launched in 1939, Rolling Rock has always been associated with the number 33. The reasons for this are shrouded in mystery. Various theories have attempted to explain it, but no definitive answer is known – at least it provides something to think about while enjoying the beer's crisp, sweet, refreshing flavour.

The Latrobe Brewing Company was established in 1893 in the small town of Latrobe in the foothills of Pennsylvania's Allegheny Mountains. The brewery closed for a few years during Prohibition, but reopened when it was purchased by the five Tito brothers, Frank, Joseph, Robert, Ralph and Anthony, who quickly set about devising a new recipe to cater for changing beer tastes, eventually coming up with Rolling Rock, which was named in honour of the tumbling streams full of pebbles that supplied the brewery with water.

SPECIFICATIONS
Brewery: Latrobe
Location: Latrobe, PA
Style: Lager
Colour: Bright golden yellow
Alcohol: 4.6%
Serving temperature: 6°–8°C (42.8°–46.4°F)
Food: Pork pie

Oregon Honey Beer

Oregon Honey Beer comes from the MacTarnahan's brewery, which produces MacTarnahan's Scottish-style beers, but this one has more of a genuine homegrown character to its flavours and aromas.

Oregon Honey Beer is a crisp and refreshing ale with a hint of sweetness provided by the addition of clover honey. The beer also has a soft, mellow, malty character balanced by the judicious use of Williamette hops. It is ideal as a light, easy-drinking summer beer, in stark contrast to another of the brewery's beers, MacFrost, a strong, rich winter beer made with five types of malt and aromatized and bittered with three varieties of hops, or the MacTarnahan's Black Watch Cream Porter, which uses malted barley, unmalted grains and oatmeal.

SPECIFICATIONS
Brewery: MacTarnahan's
Location: Portland, OR
Style: American pale ale
Colour: Pale golden straw yellow
Alcohol: 4.2%
Serving temperature: 8°–10°C (46°–50°F)
Food: Shellfish

Celis White

Pierre Celis started his hugely influential brewing career in the Belgian town of Hoegaarden in 1966, producing the famous cloudy wheat beer of that name, flavoured with herbs and spices.

After the Hoegaarden brewery's sale to Interbrew, Celis moved to the United States to take part in the brewing revolution that was introducing more characterful beers to a nation raised on bland lager. Celis White is close to the original Hoegaarden (qv) recipe, brewed with coriander spice and orange peel for a light, refreshing taste, with a natural cloudy haze and deep foaming head. It went out of production for a few years, but has been revived by the Michigan Brewing Company with Celis's blessing.

SPECIFICATIONS
Brewery: Michigan
Location: Webberville, MI
Style: Belgian wheat beer
Colour: Hazy copper-orange
Alcohol: 4.9%
Serving temperature: 8°–10°C (46.4°–50°F)
Food: Spicy American-style pizza

New Glarus Wisconsin Belgian Red

Unlike many fruit beers that are flavoured with preserved fruit or syrups, this Belgian-style wheat beer has whole locally grown Montmorency cherries added during brewing to give it the finished product a genuine cherry flavour and colour.

This is hardly surprising, as New Glarus is a brewery that does not take shortcuts. After brewing, Wisconsin Belgian Red is given a lengthy period of maturation in oak tanks, and aged Hallertau hops are added for extra aroma. The brewers suggest serving this beer as an aperitif in Champagne flutes as an alternative to a sparkling wine because of its high level of carbonation and its complex and intensely fruity flavours and aromas, and with its bright red colouring it certainly looks the part.

SPECIFICATIONS
Brewery: New Glarus
Location: New Glarus, WI
Style: Fruit beer
Colour: Ruby red
Alcohol: 5.1%
Serving temperature: 10°–12°C (50°–53.6°F)
Food: Strawberries

Tuppers' Hop Pocket Ale

A hop pocket is a long sack into which hops are packed after drying – an appropriate name for this hop-laden ale and its counterpart pilsener. The ale has a powerfully floral hoppy aroma with a solid malt background; the pilsener has intensely fruity hop character.

Both are named after the man who devised the recipes, Bob Tupper, a school history teacher who also holds lectures and beer tastings at the famous Brickskeller bar in Washington, DC. They are brewed by the Old Dominion Brewing Company, in operation since 1989 and producing a wide range of hand-crafted lagers, ales and stouts, including many traditional seasonal specialities. Its beers are all brewed according to the ancient German Reinheitsgebot purity laws.

SPECIFICATIONS
Brewery: Old Dominion
Location: Ashburn, VA
Style: Pale ale
Colour: Deep golden amber
Alcohol: 6.0%
Serving temperature: 10°C (50°F)
Food: Chicken salad

Pabst (Heileman's) Old Style

Old Style is the Chicago version of Pabst beer, a clean refreshing lager with a light malty flavour.

It was originally launched in 1902, brewed by a German immigrant by the name of Gottlieb Heileman at his small brewery in the town of La Crosse, Wisconsin. The popularity of his beer quickly spread across state lines, and Old Style was soon adopted by the people of Chicago as their own brand, which led to the sponsorship of the Chicago Cubs baseball team, an association that endures to this day. Heileman Brewery became part of the Pabst family in 2000. The beer has also given its name to a design font, which was created specifically for the Pabst Brewing Company by the American typographer Frederic Goudy.

SPECIFICATIONS
Brewery: Pabst
Location: San Antonio, TX
Style: Lager
Colour: Deep golden
Alcohol: 4.5%

Serving temperature: 6°–8°C (43°–46°F)
Food: Chicago-style pizza

Pennsylvania Penn Gold Lager

Proud brewers of authentic German beers, Pennsylvania Brewing Company was founded in 1986.

All of the equipment and ingredients used in the brewery are imported from Germany, and naturally all the beers are brewed according to the ancient German Reinheitsgebot purity laws. Penn Gold is a medium-bodied Munich-style lager with a full malty flavour and a delicate hop aroma. There is also a dark version of the beer, again brewed to a style typical of the city of Munich, with a good balance of soft fruit and dark, slightly burnt malt flavours, plus a subtle dose of hops.

SPECIFICATIONS
Brewery: Pennsylvania
Location: Pittsburgh, PA
Style: Munich lager
Colour: Pale golden
Alcohol: 5.0%

Serving temperature: 8°–10°C (46°–50°F)
Food: Battered fish and freshly squeezed lemon

Pike Pale Ale

This highly quaffable pale ale provides a well-balanced blend of flavours featuring a smooth, fruity maltiness that contrasts with a fresh, floral, herby hop character.

It is the flagship beer of Pike Brewing and Pub, which started out in 1989, brewing its own beer in tiny premises in the storefront of the LaSalle hotel building in Seattle's Pike Place market. In 1996, to meet popular demand, a new, larger brewery opened just two blocks away, enabling the brewery to greatly extend its range, which includes seasonal and one-off beers. New beers included Naughty Nellie's Ale, like a soft, easy-drinking English mild, and KiltLifter, a Scottish-style 'wee heavy' with rich toasted malt flavours.

SPECIFICATIONS	
Brewery: Pike	**Alcohol:** 5.3%
Location: Seattle, WA	**Serving temperature:** 13°C (55.4°F)
Style: Pale ale	**Food:** Grilled salmon or mussel stew
Colour: Deep amber	

Redhook ESB

The Pacific Northwest is home to the United States' major hop-growing regions and many of its finest craft brewers. Redhook is one of the very earliest, established in 1981 to provide a home-grown alternative to quality imported European beers.

It was the start of a new movement in small-scale brewing that has since gained huge momentum. The first Redhook ale was modelled after dark, spicy Belgian-style abbey beers and was given a mixed reception. Redhook then launched Ballard Bitter, which proved much more popular. By far the most successful of the brewery's beers to date is its ESB, the first American beer to use the term, which it borrowed from Fuller's of London to describe its strong, complex and well-balanced bitter. Hops dominate the aroma; on the palate toasted malt flavours lead to a soft, sweet lingering finish tempered by floral hop bitterness.

SPECIFICATIONS	
Brewery: Redhook	**Alcohol:** 5.8%
Location: Woodinville, WA	**Serving temperature:** 10°–13°C (50°–55.4°F)
Style: Strong/extra special bitter	**Food:** Roast pheasant or other game
Colour: Copper	

Rogue Shakespeare Stout

Unlike the typically dry, bitter character of Irish stout, oatmeal stout has a much sweeter flavour.

Rogue's award-winning version is made with several different types of malt, including crystal and chocolate malts, roasted barley and rolled oats, which give it an opaquely dark black colouring and a rich, creamy head when poured. The aroma is predominantly characterized by ripe dark fruit such as plums or figs, with background hints of chocolate. The sweet maltiness continues to exert itself on the palate with dark roasted coffee and dry, hoppy bitterness coming in towards the finish. Shakespeare Stout received a welcome accreditation in 1994 when it took a score of 99 at the World Beer Championships, the top score of 309 beers in 44 categories. *Men's Journal* (June/July 1998) placed the stout in the category of the '100 Best Things to Eat in America'.

SPECIFICATIONS
Brewery: Rogue
Location: Newport, OR
Style: Oatmeal stout
Colour: Ebony black
Alcohol: 6%
Serving temperature: 13°C (55.4°F)
Food: Home-made pizza or a fresh green salad

Miller Genuine Draft

Frederick John Miller started brewing in his native Germany in 1849 before emigrating to the United States, where in 1855 he bought the Plank Road Brewery in Milwaukee and started brewing beer using yeast that he had brought with him from Germany.

Miller has gone on to become the United States' second-largest brewer and a household name. Miller Genuine Draft is produced at Miller's state-of-the-art brewing facility in Eden, North Carolina, using an exclusive cold-filtering process. Originally introduced in 1986, it has a light, grainy malt aroma, a slightly sweet and sharp flavour and a smooth, dry, lightly hopped finish. A version with a reduced alcohol content, Miller Genuine Draft Light, is also available.

SPECIFICATIONS
Brewery: SAB Miller
Location: Milwaukee, WI
Style: Lager
Colour: Bright, clear gold / yellow
Alcohol: 4.6%
Serving temperature: 6°–8°C (42.8°–46.4°F)
Food: Barbecued meats

Miller Lite

The first mainstream 'light' beer, this carefully crafted pilsener uses the finest ingredients and brewing techniques to produce a rich, full-bodied taste at only 96 calories.

From the bottle, the beer pours a pale straw golden colour, topped with a white head. There is not a great deal of aroma, although there is a hint of sweet cereal grains. The brew is light bodied, with a thin but refreshing texture. There is a flavour of adjuncts (cream corn, cereal) with virtually no hop presence. Miller Lite is a good thirst-quenching beer. Some beer experts might criticize Miller Lite on the grounds that it is a little bland, but it is eminently drinkable and definitely one to have in hand while relaxing in the shade.

SPECIFICATIONS
Brewery: SAB Miller
Location: Milwaukee, WI
Style: Pilsener
Colour: Yellow
Alcohol: 4.2%
Serving temperature: 6°–8°C (43°–46°F)
Food: Chicken, fish

Sierra Nevada Bigfoot

Sierra Nevada is perhaps the most famous of all the new generation of craft brewers operating in the United States today.

From a brewery established in 1979 by Ken Grosman, the beers were an instant hit. It was not long before this tiny brewery was struggling to keep up with demand, and in 1989 a new brewery was opened built with equipment imported from Germany, including traditional copper mash kettles. The beers are justifiably renowned for the copious amounts of hops used in creating them, and Bigfoot Ale is no exception. This award-winning beer is a fine example of a traditional barley wine with an intensely fruity aroma, a dense mouth-filling body and a deep rich complex flavour that provides a superb balance between forthright maltiness and an intensely bitter, resiny, citrus hop character.

SPECIFICATIONS
Brewery: Sierra Nevada
Location: Chico, CA
Style: Barley wine
Colour: Deep red-brown
Alcohol: 9.6%
Serving temperature: 14°–16°C (57°–60°F)
Food: Turkey and Christmas pudding

Stone Ruination IPA

'A liquid poem to the glory of hops' proclaims the label of Stone's Ruination IPA, while the devilish figure hints at the powerful flavours that reside within the bottle.

Even by the standards of a brewery that is known for its love of hops, this is a particularly hoppy beer with an intensely bitter flavour (rated at more than 100 IBUs/International Bitterness Units) which aims to have a 'ruining' effect on your palate – hence the name. The strong flavour of Stone Ruination is backed up by an equally strong 7.7% alcohol content, making it well above the more typical 5–5.5% regions of IPAs. More moderate than Stone Ruination is Stone Smoked Porter, a smooth, silky dark beer with robust chocolate and coffee-like flavours and a hint of whisky-like smokiness that comes from the use of selected malts roasted over peat.

SPECIFICATIONS
Brewery: Stone
Location: San Marcos, CA
Style: India pale ale
Colour: Bright, pale amber
Alcohol: 7.7%
Serving temperature: 10°–12°C (50°–53.6°F)
Food: Fried seafood

Yuengling Traditional Lager

D.G. Yuengling & Son, commonly called Yuengling, is the oldest operating brewing company in the United States, established in 1829. Yuengling Traditional lager is the company's flagship beer.

This lager, available bottled or on tap, pours a clear amber with a white head. The aroma is mildly bready, with hints of almost caramel-like malts and a bit of floral hops. The flavour is much the same; bready, a touch sweet, and with an undertone of hops. This is a beer that can be consumed in considerable quantity without becoming cloying, unlike some other lagers. It has a good colour compared to Miller and Bud, and there is a hint of light fruitiness that is compatible with the hops, in both the aroma and taste. Many drinkers class this as the best beer of its class in North America; it is certainly the most common in western Pennsylvania.

SPECIFICATIONS
Brewery: D.G. Yuengling & Son
Location: Pottsville, PA
Style: Pale lager
Colour: Amber
Alcohol: 4.9%
Serving temperature: 6°–8°C (43°–46°F)
Food: Any cold meats, fish, chicken

Latin American and Caribbean Beers

Before the arrival of the Europeans in the sixteenth century, beer was unknown in Latin America. Civilizations such as the Aztecs, Incas and Mayans had traditions for drinking fermented maize beverages, while in the Caribbean native populations brewed maize to make drinks that varied in recipe from island to island.

The Aztecs created drinks from the leaves and juice of the agave plant, too, including a simple brew called *pulque*, drunk for medicinal and religious reasons. When the conquistadors arrived, they introduced the process of distillation, which led to the creation of mezcal, which soon became the most popular drink in Latin America and a valuable commodity.

The conquistadors set up many small breweries across the continent, but it was not until the arrival of refrigeration in the late nineteenth century, and the introduction of golden lagers by Bavarian, Swiss and Austrian brewers, that beer became truly popular. Later on, when prohibition hit North America, the sleepy border town of Tijuana in Mexico became a popular refuge for those looking for a drink, creating a lasting legacy for the Mexican brewing industry, making it by far the largest brewing nation in Latin America.

Latin America's next-largest brewing country is Brazil, where a notable addition to the usual range of golden lagers is a distinctive black beer, brewed using roasted barley and a blend of dark indigenous grains, as well as lupins for aroma.

Strong, sweet lagers are also the mainstay of Caribbean drinking, but stout is very popular throughout the region as well.

Left: The people of Latin America and the Caribbean are noted for their love of beer as much as for their love of life. As well as brewing quality distinctive lagers and beers for the domestic market, the region has become one of the largest beer exporting territories in the world, building popularity through brands such as Sol, Corona Extra and Red Stripe.

Above: Latin America, like any other world region, has some state-of-the-art brewing facilities. It has also seen the continuation of traditional brewing among many of the smaller companies.

STATISTICS

Total production: 223,990,000 hectolitres (5,917,190,000 gallons) per year

Consumption per capita: 55 litres (15 gallons) per year

Famous breweries: Bucanero Cervecería; Cervecería Cuauhtémoc; Cervecería Modelo; Cervecería y Maltería Quilmes; Desnoes & Geddes; Especialidad Cerveceras

Famous brands: Dos Equis; Igúazu; Mayabe Calidad Extra; Quilmes; Red Stripe; Sol

Dos Equis

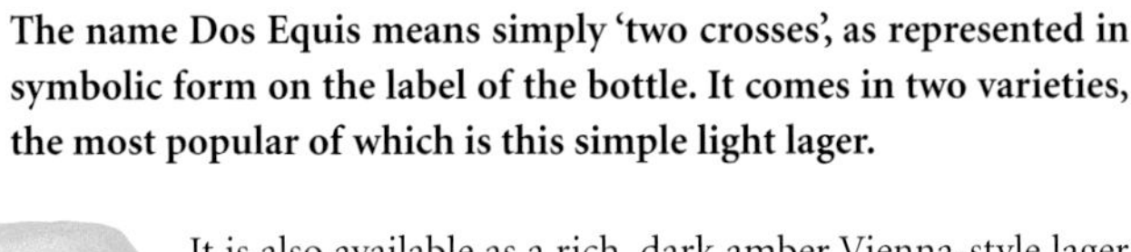

The name Dos Equis means simply 'two crosses', as represented in symbolic form on the label of the bottle. It comes in two varieties, the most popular of which is this simple light lager.

It is also available as a rich, dark amber Vienna-style lager (Dos Equis Amber) with a sweet, fruity malt flavour and hints of chocolate. Dos Equis is currently one of the leading brands of Mexico's largest brewer, Cervecería Cuauhtémoc, which was founded in 1890 by two Spanish men, Isaac Heron and Jose Calderón. The brewery's first beer was Carta Blanca, a sparkling beer which was originally packaged in corked bottles.

SPECIFICATIONS

Brewery: Cervecería Cuauhtémoc Moctezuma (FEMSA)
Location: Monterrey, Mexico
Style: Vienna lager
Colour: Golden amber-yellow
Alcohol: 4.8%
Serving temperature: 6°–8°C (42.8°–46.4°F)
Food: Grilled white fish

Sol

One of the most famous Mexican beer brands, Sol is a light, refreshing lager brewed for a smoother, fuller body.

It has a fruity malt aroma and a hoppy bitterness on the palate that gives it an invigorating dryness. It is presented in a clear bottle, allowing its vibrant golden yellow colour to shine out, and this is what gives the beer its name (Sol is Spanish for 'sun'). In the 1980s, Sol found widespread popularity in Europe and the United States, as well as in its domestic market. Other brands from the group include Tecate, launched in 1944 in the city that gives the beer its name as a light, thirst-quenching beer with a fairly low alcohol content, making it ideal for Mexico's hot climate.

SPECIFICATIONS

Brewery: Cervecería Cuauhtémoc Moctezuma (FEMSA)
Location: Monterrey, Mexico
Style: Lager
Colour: Clear golden yellow
Alcohol: 4.6%
Serving temperature: 5°–7°C (41°–44.6°F)
Food: Steak and sautéed potatoes

Casta Bruna

Casta Bruna is a smooth and well-balanced English-style pale ale. It possesses a delicate floral aroma in which hints of toffee sweetness are apparent.

Four types of pale roasted malts and English hops give Casta Bruna a medium body and a complex range of flavours, including notes of chocolate, peaches and a herbal hop bitterness. The excellent range of quality ales from the craft brewer Especialidad Cerveceras also includes the vigorously aromatic Casta Dorada, brewed in the style of Belgium's strong golden ales, while Casta Milenia is a limited-edition vintage ale in the tradition of the strong Belgian abbey beers, bottled with unfermented wort to create a beer that improves with extended cellaring. Casta Morena is a dark ale, and Casta Triguera a wheat beer.

SPECIFICATIONS

Brewery: Especialidad Cerveceras
Location: Apodaca, Mexico
Style: English pale ale
Colour: Copper red-brown
Alcohol: 5.4%
Serving temperature: 10°–12°C (50°–53.6°F)
Food: Pasta with tomato-based sauces

Pacifico Clara

Pacifico Clara is part of the extensive range of beers from the Modelo brewery of Mexico City, although it is mostly produced at the company's subsidiary Pacific Brewery in Mazatlán, Sinaloa, in the north of Mexico.

It is a subtle, refined beer with a vigorous carbonation and a light, well-balanced flavour. As well as its famous Corona and Modelo beer ranges, the brewery produces several other brands, notably including Victoria. This is a malty Vienna-style lager that was originally brewed by the Toluca brewery, one of Mexico's oldest breweries which was founded in 1865 and acquired by Modelo in 1935.

SPECIFICATIONS

Brewery: Cervecería Modelo
Location: Mexico City, Mexico
Style: Pilsener
Colour: Golden yellow
Alcohol: 4.5%
Serving temperature: 7°C (44.6°F)
Food: Sharp, spicy dishes

Mayabe Calidad Extra

One of the largest towns in Cuba, Holguin lies close to the spot on the coast where Christopher Columbus first landed in 1492. It is also home to the Bucanero brewery, which produces Cerveza Cristal lager, the best-selling beer brand in Cuba.

Bucanero specializes in easy-drinking lagers and Mayabe Calidad Extra is the brewery's 'premium' brand, brewed slightly stronger and with a smoother body. It has a light, uncomplicated, slightly sweet, grainy flavour. Another stronger version is called Mayabe Calidad Extra Fuerte, and the range includes a clear golden pilsener-style beer called Palma Cristal.

SPECIFICATIONS

Brewery: Bucanero Cervecería
Location: Holguin, Cuba
Style: Lager
Colour: Pale straw yellow
Alcohol: 5%
Serving temperature: 5°–7°C (41°–44.6°F)
Food: Fried fish and seafood

Red Stripe

Red Stripe is a pale golden strong lager with a full malty flavour balanced by a light hop aroma and refreshingly dry, bitter finish. It comes from the Desnoes & Geddes brewery, established in 1918.

At first, the company produced only soft drinks, but turned to brewing in 1927. The first Red Stripe was a rich, flavourful ale, but was replaced in 1938 with the golden lager that we know today. In recent years, Desnoes & Geddes has entered into arrangements with Heineken that have seen its beers exported and in some cases brewed overseas, making it one of the few breweries in the Caribbean to enjoy a truly worldwide reputation.

SPECIFICATIONS

Brewery: Desnoes & Geddes
Location: Kingston, Jamaica
Style: Lager
Colour: Pale golden yellow
Alcohol: 4.7%
Serving temperature: 6°–7°C (42.8°–44.6°F)
Food: Fried seafood and saffron rice

Igúazu

Igúazu is one of a wide range of beers originating from the Quilmes brewery of Buenos Aires in Argentina.

It takes its name from a spectacular horseshoe-shaped waterfall, 80 m (260 ft) high and nearly three kilometres (two miles) across, that is famous outside Argentina for having featured in the Robert de Niro film *The Mission*. In local dialect the name, unsurprisingly, means 'big water'. Igúazu is a bottom-fermented golden lager with a light grainy flavour and a subtle hop aroma. Other products in the Quilmes range include alcohol-free Liberty, and a pair of beers reflecting the brewery's German origins: Bock and a wheat beer called Andes.

SPECIFICATIONS

Brewery: Cervecería y Maltería Quilmes
Location: Buenos Aires, Argentina
Style: Lager
Colour: Golden yellow
Alcohol: 4.9%
Serving temperature: 6°–8°C (42.8°–46.4°F)
Food: Salads and cheese

Quilmes

The Quilmes brewery and maltery was founded in Buenos Aires' Quilmes district in 1888 by German immigrant Otto Bemberg. The name has gone on to become synonymous in Argentina with beer.

Expansion throughout the early twentieth century saw the brewery become one of the biggest businesses of any type in Buenos Aires, with its beers being exported far and wide, including to Europe, and Quilmes has even gone on to become the official sponsor of the Argentine national football team. The brewery's main product is this clear golden lager, which has a light malty flavour.

SPECIFICATIONS

Brewery: Cervecería y Maltería Quilmes
Location: Buenos Aires, Argentina
Style: Lager
Colour: Pale golden yellow
Alcohol: 4.9%
Serving temperature: 6°–8°C (42.8°–46.4°F)
Food: Potato chips

VIKING
bjór

Icelandic Beers

Of all the Scandinavian countries, Iceland has the shortest brewing tradition, at least in the legal sense. In the past, Iceland was allowed to produce only 2.2% abv (alcohol by volume) beers, and that particular law was repealed only a few years ago. The two principal brews are Viking and Thule.

On the first day of March every year Icelanders celebrate 'Beer Day', a tradition that began on 1 March 1989 when prohibition was lifted. It makes for a wild 24 hours in Reykjavik, the capital. Centuries ago, Icelanders restricted bouts of really heavy drinking to times of feasting. One of the biggest feasts was Thorrablot, which took place in February – the fourth month of winter in the Icelandic calendar. At this time the Vikings consumed huge quantities of such delicacies as *svid* (parboiled lamb's head), fermented shark meat and pickled ram's testicles. It is no wonder they needed lots of strong ale and mead to wash it all down.

During World War II, British, then American, forces occupied Iceland. This gave Icelanders a chance to sidestep prohibition for a few years and sample a selection of foreign beers. Then came 1944, the year Iceland severed its union with Denmark to become a sovereign state, an event that was soon followed by the departure of the Allied forces, except for a strong US presence that was maintained during the Cold War era. Once again, Iceland was plunged into a wilderness of enforced abstinence that lasted for years until the resurgence of brewing today. The trouble is that Icelandic beer is so expensive people cannot afford to drink much of it. But Icelanders persist in their claim that it is well worth drinking, if only because of the purity of the water that goes into it.

Left: Viking is the best-selling beer in Iceland, and Icelanders are proud of the purity of the water used in the brewing process. Produced in Akureyri, in the north of the country, Viking is fast increasing its market share. The high taxes charged on all alcoholic drinks in Iceland mean, however, that an evening spent sampling the local brews in Reykjavik is likely to prove an expensive night out.

Above: Egill Skalagrímsson Brewery (seen above) was founded in 1913 by Tómas Tómasson. In addition to beer, the company produces a range of popular soft drinks.

STATISTICS

Total production: 120,000 hectolitres (3,170,000 gallons) per year
Consumption per capita: 56 litres (15 gallons) per year
Famous breweries: Egill; Viking
Famous brands: Egils Pilsner; Viking Thule

Egils Pilsner

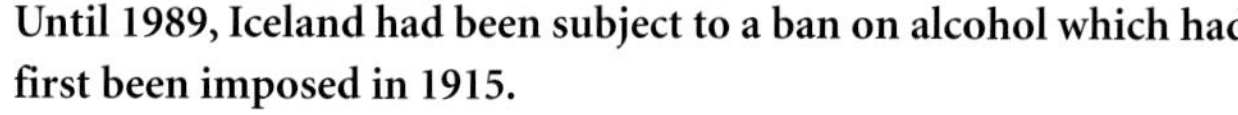

Until 1989, Iceland had been subject to a ban on alcohol which had first been imposed in 1915.

Throughout that period, the tiny country's few breweries, such as Egill Skalagrímsson of Reykjavik, concentrated on producing soft drinks, which still make up a large part of its business today, and low-alcohol beers, including Egils Malt, which has only 1% alcohol. Egill's light version of a pilsener-style lager is not much stronger than this; however, it is brewed with pure Icelandic water to give it a clean, refreshing flavour. Both the brewery and its beers take their names from the Egils saga, the story of a tenth-century Icelandic warrior and poet named Egill Skalagrímsson.

SPECIFICATIONS
Brewery: Egill Skalagrímsson
Location: Iceland
Style: Lager
Colour: Golden yellow
Alcohol: 2.2%
Serving temperature: 6°–7°C (42.8°–44.6°F)
Food: Salads

Egils Maltbjór

As its name implies, Egils Maltbjór is a dark, malty brew that is quite satisfying to the palate. It makes a refreshing change from the other types of lager produced by this brewery.

The beer has a slightly pungent aroma, which is probably accounted for by the quality of the hops that are used in the brewing process. Its appearance is pleasing, with the beer's chestnut colour being topped by a small head. Overall, Egils Maltbjór is reminiscent of the Danish Maltøl variety, which may indeed have inspired it. Some critics have hailed Egils Maltbjór as the best of the Icelandic beers that they have sampled, but this may simply be because it is different from the more usual styles of pilsener that are to be readily found on every supermarket shelf. Other products in the range include Egils Malt Jólabjór and Egils Malt Paskabjór.

SPECIFICATIONS
Brewery: Egill Skalagrímsson
Location: Reykjavik
Style: Bock
Colour: Reddish brown
Alcohol: 5.6%
Serving temperature: 10°C (50°F)
Food: Meat pies, roasts

Viking Lager

Viking is a sweetish lager with a hint of malt. It is a pilsener type, with a very small, light and creamy head.

The aroma on pouring this premium golden lager is very pleasant, but it dissipates rather quickly. The lager is slightly sticky, which is a by-product of the corn that goes into the brewing process. The pure Icelandic water and a unique combination of malt, hops, maize and sugar provide the beer with a distinct bitter taste, and the overall effect is similar to Carlsberg. Still, there is no escaping the fact that Icelandic beer is an expensive proposition, this being a side effect of high taxation, with imported beers naturally being more costly than the varieties brewed locally. Viking is gradually but surely increasing its share of the beer market in Iceland. It is the best-selling beer in the country's state-run monopoly shops, and it is also very popular in restaurants and pubs in its draught form.

SPECIFICATIONS
Brewery: Viking
Location: Akureyri
Style: Pilsener
Colour: Pale gold
Alcohol: 4.6%
Serving temperature: 6°–8°C (43°–46°F)
Food: Fish, cold meats

Viking Thule

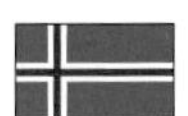

Viking Thule, the second of the Viking brewery's popular beers, is a typically Icelandic brew, characterized by a pale golden colour and a small, white head.

One of this beer's best qualities is its aromatic, hoppy nose. Extremely light-bodied, it has only the slightest touch of malt and hops. Far from being just another boring example of Scandinavian beer, it is a beautifully fresh and thirst-quenching drink. There is only a hint of bitterness, which might displease some critics, and it has certainly been criticized on the grounds that it is slightly cloudy. The beer derives its name from history. Thule is the ancient name for Iceland. The landmass was discovered by the seafarer Pytheas of Massalia, in 325 BC, so it is said, after six days' sailing from the island of Britain. The real Thule, in fact, was probably Greenland.

SPECIFICATIONS
Brewery: Viking
Location: Akureyri
Style: Lager
Colour: Pale gold
Alcohol: 5.0%
Serving temperature: 6°–7°C (43°–45°F)
Food: Fish and shellfish, snacks

Norwegian Beers

Think of Norwegian industry, and things that spring immediately to mind are farming, forestry, fisheries and shipping. Brewing is something that might easily be passed over. Yet after many years in the doldrums, the Norwegian brewing industry is taking on a new lease of life.

In Norway, brewing beer is a regional affair, with few national brews. The country boasts the world's most northerly brewery, at Tromsø inside the Arctic Circle. The Norwegian brewing industry suffers, however, from high taxation and a mass of regulations. In fact, it operates under the strictest regulation of any in Europe. Much of this has to do with a very active anti-alcohol lobby, which exerts a strong influence on the government. Over the past few years, the industry has been consolidated into one large multi-national group, one indigenous group and a few independents. Most of the beer brewed is for home consumption; some Norwegian beers are exported, but the trade is insignificant.

By the 1990s, the Norwegian beer market was dominated by Ringnes, which achieved control by buying up smaller concerns and then closing them down. Eventually, they formed an alliance with Carlsberg of Denmark and Pripps of Sweden, so that by the late 1990s 85% of the industry was in the hands of the two biggest brewing groups, Carlsberg-Ringnes and Hansa-Borg.

Compounding the brewers' problems in Norway is the law that forbids any beer greater than 4.75% alcohol to be sold anywhere other than in the state-controlled Vinmonopol stores.

Left: Customers pack a busy tavern set on the old wharf of Bryggen in Bergen. Norwegian beer drinkers have to enjoy their drink under a cloud of quite severe government regulation, which controls everything from the price of the drink (through imposition of taxes) down the the alcoholic content. Nevertheless, Norwegian breweries still manage to produce some excellent beers.

Above: A label from the Hansa brewery, proudly declaring its heritage. Established in 1891, Hansa is today one of the oldest breweries in Norway. It was also the first Norwegian brewery to export to the USA.

STATISTICS

Total production: 2,230,000 hectolitres (59,000,000 gallons) per year
Consumption per capita: 55 litres (14.5 gallons) per year
Famous breweries: Aass; Hansa; Ringnes
Famous brands: Aass Pils; Hansa Premium

Aass Bayer

Aass is Norway's oldest brewery, having started as a general trading company in 1834 with a bakery and a small brewery as sidelines. It was burnt down in a disastrous fire in 1866. After rebuilding, however, it was re-established on a much more successful commercial footing and on a far larger scale than its predecessor.

A dark, nutty brew, Aass Bayer gets consistently good reviews in the beer guides. Bayer has a distinctive hoppy taste, with a hint of caramel or chocolate. Despite its deep and rich appearance it has quite a 'thin' taste, which may come as a surprise to drinkers expecting a more full-bodied brew. It is a beer that can be readily enjoyed on its own, but it is at its best when drunk with fairly heavy food such as sausages and game. Aass Bayer is probably the best 'all round' Norwegian beer, and is a popular supermarket purchase.

SPECIFICATIONS
Brewery: Aass Bryggeri
Location: Drammen
Style: Dark lager
Colour: Amber
Alcohol: 4.5%
Serving temperature: 15°C (60°F)
Food: Sausages, pickles

Aass Bock

Aass Bock is a dark lager produced in accordance with Norway's very strict purity laws. It is brewed from malted barley produced only in the Scandinavian countries, and is one of the best bocks available outside Germany.

The brewery uses the famous Sazer and Hallertau hops from Germany. Aass Bock is brewed in cool temperatures and allowed to mature for three months before bottling. As well as cans, it is sold in an attractive brown bottle containing 330 ml (11.2 fl oz). One of the stronger Norwegian lagers, Aass Bock has a smooth and creamy mouthfeel that sits easily on the palate, and is readily distinguished from other dark lagers.

SPECIFICATIONS
Brewery: Aass Bryggeri
Location: Drammen
Style: Dark lager
Colour: Dark brown
Alcohol: 5.9%
Serving temperature: 10–12°C (50–53°F)
Food: Dish, cheese, cooked meats, dark bread

Hansa Premium

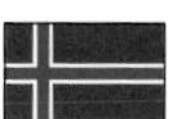

This is a pale gold, clear beer with a sharp aroma. It is slightly malty to the palate with the flavour of hops coming through distinctly. It pours well, with a large white head that lasts quite a while.

There is wheat in the flavour, which is rather unusual for a beer of this kind. All in all, it is an enjoyable, thirst-quenching summer drink. The Hansa brewery spent a brief time in Swedish hands, having been purchased by Procordia in 1989, but six years later it was bought back by a group of Norwegian investors and merged with Borg to form Hansa Borg Bryggerier, Norway's largest independent brewery group.

SPECIFICATIONS
Brewery: Hansa Bryggeri
Location: Bergen
Style: Pale lager
Colour: Pale gold

Alcohol: 4.5%
Serving temperature: 6–7°C (43–45°F)
Food: Cold meats, fish

Ringnes Pils

Norwegian beer is the product of a rich tradition of brewing in Norway, despite high taxation and stringent rules, governing when and where alcoholic beverages may be sold, that make Norway somewhat of a harsh climate for beer drinkers. Currently, Carlsberg-Ringnes is one of two large brewers dominating the Norwegian beer market.

Most of their output is in the form of pale lager-style beers such as Pilsner and Fatøl which are widely available and very popular. Bayerøl, a kind of dark lager, slightly sweeter than German dark lagers, is also readily available.

SPECIFICATIONS
Brewery: Ringnes Bryggeri
Location: Oslo
Style: Pilsener
Colour: Golden

Alcohol: 4.7%
Serving temperature: 6–7°C (43–45°F)
Food: Potato crisps

SPENDRUP'S
Vi säljer
Kodak film

Swedish Beers

From the Middle Ages until the seventeenth century, beer was Sweden's national drink. From 1700 onwards, however, it rapidly lost its popularity to spirits. Breweries had the exclusive right to distil and, given the large sums to be earned from spirits, had little incentive to develop the brewing side of their business.

Unsurprisingly, the industry went into decline. Before the middle of the nineteenth century a wide range of styles was produced. The three most common indigenous styles (or Svenskøl) were *dubbelt øl* (double beer), *enkelt øl* (single beer) and *svagøl* (weak beer). All these were top-fermented. The initial stimulus that helped beer to regain popularity came from abroad. Porter was imported from Britain throughout the eighteenth century, and in 1791 William Knox founded Sweden's first porter brewery in Göteborg.

The most important nineteenth-century development was the introduction of bottom-fermenting beer by Fredrik Rosenquist of Åkershult. He had travelled through Germany studying brewing methods. On his return to Sweden, he rented a small brewery in Stockholm, and in late 1843 marketed Sweden's first lager, a dark beer in the Munich style. Other breweries imitated Rosenquist's beer, and soon a distinct Swedish style of *lageröl* developed. Pale brown or dark amber, it was relatively lightly hopped with an alcohol content of around 5.5%. Many Swedish breweries still make a *bayerskt* in this approximate style. Throughout the second half of the last century this and porter were the standard beer types.

Pilsener was introduced in the 1870s. There was some initial resistance to the high levels of bitterness, and it was first marketed among the middle classes. Gradually, other breweries in Stockholm, then in the rest of Sweden, began to brew Pilseners of their own. By the end of World War I it was the dominant style.

Left: A crowded bar seen in the historic square of Stortorget in Stockholm. The brewing industry was revived in Sweden during the nineteenth century after a long period of neglect, and today it produces a broad range of brews from light and refreshing pilseners through to dark and strong porters.

STATISTICS

Total production: 3,788,000 hectolitres (100,000,000 gallons) per year
Consumption per capita: 51.5 litres (13.5 gallons) per year
Famous breweries: Carlsberg Sverige; Jämtlands Bryggeri; Slottskällans Bryggeri
Famous brands: Carnegie Stark Porter; Jämtlands Heaven; Jämtlands Hell; Slottskällans Imperial Stout

Above: A row of beers from Jämtlands, one of Sweden's most respected microbreweries, a company that has won many beer awards. Sweden's brewing industry still manages to prosper despite heavy government restrictions.

Carnegie Stark-Porter

David Carnegie was an expatriate Scot whose family had settled in Gothenburg and prospered as merchants. He first brewed a classic among Swedish beers, Carnegie Porter, in 1836, and opened the first industrial brewery in Sweden.

The label on his Porter bottles is the same today as it was then, even though the beer is now part of the Carlsberg Sverige brewery. It is now brewed at Carlsberg's Falkenberg brewery, which is on the river Ätran, using water obtained from a spring. The brew is a black, top-fermented porter of 5.5% abv. It has strong roasted tones of a chocolate character and lots of hop bitterness. Both of these strong, rich flavours are balanced and softened by a degree of sweetness. There is a complex blend of the aromas of fermentation combined with a heavy but smooth body. Carnegie Porter is classed as a vintage beer. In other words, it improves with storage.

SPECIFICATIONS
Brewery: Carlsberg Sverige
Location: Falkenberg
Style: Porter
Colour: Black

Alcohol: 5.5%
Serving temperature: 5°C (41°F)
Food: Bread and cheese, oysters

Jämtlands Heaven

This is a very dark beer which produces a small brown head. It is dry and bitter to the taste with a splendid, full aroma of hops and hardly a trace of sweetness. The strong aroma is also redolent of smoke, caramel and roasted malts.

Heaven is available in bottles or on draught; the draught has a slightly lighter, dark reddish-brown colour. Jämtlands is a microbrewery and is situated in the town of Pilgrimstad in north-central Sweden, not far from Östersund.

SPECIFICATIONS
Brewery: Jämtlands Bryggeri
Location: Pilgrimstad
Style: Schwarzbier
Colour: Black

Alcohol: 5.0%
Serving Temperature: 10°C (50°F)
Food: Cold meats

Jämtlands Hell

This beer pours with a small head and is golden coloured, with a malty, fruity aroma and notes of yeast. There are hops in the aroma, too, and these are noticeable in the flavour, which is a little on the bitter side. This is a very well balanced and popular lager.

The Jämtlands Brewery is one of the smallest breweries in Sweden. It was first established in January 1996. The brewery has an annual capacity of 350,000 litres (92,500 gallons) of beer, and in just a decade has expanded its activities to produce a range of beers to suit all tastes. The malts used in Jämtlands beer are of the highest quality and are imported from England as well as being purchased in Sweden.

SPECIFICATIONS
Brewery: Jämtlands Bryggeri
Location: Pilgrimstad, Sweden
Style: Premium lager
Colour: Golden
Alcohol: 5.1%
Serving Temperature: 6°–8°C (43°–46°F)
Food: Seafood

Slottskällans Imperial Stout

This stout is a good, strong, dark drink from the Slottskällans microbrewery that pours a clear brown, shining ruby colour when held to the light. It has a lasting tan head that shows some excellent lacing on the glass.

The aroma is of artificial chocolate, yeast and grape skins, while the taste is chocolate, grape skins, liquorice, peppery alcohol, apples and some other fruit. It is medium-bodied and a little chalky on the palate, but has great flavours that contrast perfectly with one another. Many of the products of this microbrewery, including Imperial Stout, have won international awards.

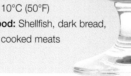

SPECIFICATIONS
Brewery: Slottskällans Bryggeri
Location: Uppsala
Style: Stout
Colour: Dark Ruby
Alcohol: 9.0%
Serving Temperature: 10°C (50°F)
Food: Shellfish, dark bread, cooked meats

KOFF
KOFF
KOFF
NK-LOGISTIIK

Finnish Beers

In Finland, the traditional art of brewing is very old, but the ancient Finnish brewing style that produces ales such as Sahti is hard to find. There is nothing like it commercially produced anywhere else in the world, although the Swedish island of Gotland and the Estonian island of Saaremaa do have local versions of their own.

Brewpubs and microbreweries are a very new thing, and micros in particular have been slow to get going, but there is an excellent one in Central Finland called Palvasalmi. The Finnish brewing industry, like that of Iceland, suffered from prohibition. In Finland's case, this lasted from 1919 to 1932. Crippling taxation has also had an adverse effect. Today, two major breweries dominate the Finnish beer market: Hartwall, with a 50% share, and Sinebrychoff. Hartwall has enjoyed real success with its Lapin Kulta, which has its roots in Finnish Lapland, and particularly with Lapin Kulta Winter, which is a seasonal brew available from November through January.

The Sinebrychoff brewery had an interesting beginning. On 13 October 1819 the Imperial Reconstruction Committee, which was appointed to create a new capital city for the Grand Duchy of Finland, granted merchant Nikolai Sinebrychoff an undeveloped block of land in the Hietalahti district of Helsinki on which to build 'a great beer factory' to meet the needs of the city. Almost the very first job was carried out by two horses, who pulled logs on a sledge over the frozen sea to Hietalahti from a house that had been taken apart on Suomenlinna, just off the coast of Helsinki. The logs were used to rebuild the house, which still stands in the corner of Sinebrychoff Park.

In 1990, the Perinteisen Oluen Seura (Finnish Society for Traditional Beers) was founded. Its goal is to increase the availability of traditional beers with a characteristic flavour at the expense of international brands such as Carlsberg, which tend to dominate the market.

Left: Trucks push out into the night carrying Koff, one of the biggest brands of the Sinebrychoff brewery. The popularity of Sinebrychoff's brews demands a fleet of nearly 300 trucks making a total delivery mileage of 59,544km (37,000 miles) on a daily basis.

Above: Lunch time on the Esplanadi Boulevard in Helsinki offers a good opportunity to sample local beers. As with most of Scandinavia, Finland has a mix of dominant major breweries and emergent small producers.

STATISTICS

Total production: 4,617,000 hectolitres (121,900,000 gallons) per year
Consumption per capita: 84 litres (22 gallons) per year
Famous breweries: Hartwall; Sinebrychoff; Lammin
Famous brands: Lapin Kulta; Koff; Finlandia Sahti

Finlandia Sahti

Sahti is a rustic style of Finnish beer and is the oldest of its kind still in production, having been brewed since about the tenth century. The name Sahti is derived from an old Germanic word meaning 'juice of the barley'.

Juniper and hops feature in the ingredients, and the beer comes either on draught or bottled. It is very strong, with an aroma of cloves. The brew tends to be sticky and sweet, which some drinkers may find unpalatable. It has a hazy amber colour and pours with a very small off-white head; the spicy aroma persists in the taste. The beer can best be described as full-bodied. Part of its attraction is that no two tasters can actually agree on what its subtle flavours are.

SPECIFICATIONS
Brewery: Finlandia Sahti Oy
Location: Matku
Style: Traditional ale
Colour: Amber
Alcohol: 8.0%
Serving temperature: 10°C (50°F)
Food: Roast meats

Lapin Kulta

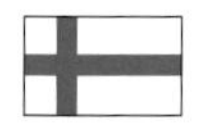

The Finnish brew of Lapin Kulta is a strong, smooth lager with a malty flavour.

Its name translates as 'Lapland's gold' and reflects the heritage of the brewery, which was founded in 1873 in the far northern Finnish town of Tornio, close to the border with Sweden, when hundreds of gold prospectors descended on the area. Both ventures proved successful – the prospectors found 130 kg (230 lb) of gold, while the brewery became a thriving business, despite Finland being hit hard by prohibition. Following an agreement with Hartwall in the 1960s the beers began to be distributed to the rest of Finland and even exported abroad. The company also produces Lapin Kulta Talviolut – Lapin Kulta Winter – a stronger, darker beer available between November and January.

SPECIFICATIONS
Brewery: Hartwall
Location: Tornio, Lapland
Style: Lager
Colour: Golden yellow
Alcohol: 7%
Serving temperature: 6°–7°C (42.8°–44.6°F)
Food: Peppered tuna steaks

Lammin Puhti

Pekka Kaarianen, who single-handedly revived the juniper-laced Sahti style in 1990, created this variation of the Lammin Sahti by replacing the Finnish baker's yeast with regular ale yeast.

In addition, Lammin Puhti is boiled in the brew kettle for some 60 minutes. Both adjustments have been made to create a variation of the original Lammin Sahti with a very robust shelf life of more than 12 months. The ale is dark orange in colour, with notes of peach, citrus and lemon on the palate. It has a rather big body with a dry, almondy finish. Lammin Puhti, rather confusingly, is also known as Lammin Kataja.

SPECIFICATIONS
Brewery: Lammin Sahti Oy
Location: Lammin
Style: Juniper ale
Colour: Dark orange

Alcohol: 5.0%
Serving Temperature: 10°C (50°F)
Food: Fruit pies

Koff

According to the brewer's publicity, you can taste almost 200 years of traditions and expertise in Koff bottled beer. The crystal-clear golden-yellow colour, full-bodied foam and unique aftertaste have all contributed to making Koff beer an internationally renowned lager and recipient of awards.

Koff is balanced, yet aromatic and full-bodied. From the same stable comes Koff Porter, a highly popular dark beer. Very black, with a dense brown head, it has an aroma that is hugely malty, roast-like and sweet. It has a big creamy body with very low carbonation. Though it is mildly sweet at first, hop bitterness creeps up in the flavour later. The lingering black finish has just a bit of papery oxidation. According to some critics, Koff Porter is preferable to Guinness, an opinion which might raise a few eyebrows.

SPECIFICATIONS
Brewery: Sinebrychoff
Location: Kerava
Style: Porter
Colour: Dark velvet

Alcohol: 7.2%
Serving temperature: 10°C (50°F)
Food: Smoked salmon, pickled herring

DE DET FØRSTE NY CARLSB

Danish Beers

Danish beer-making has long been identified with the international power of Carlsberg, with its status as one of the world's great beer producers. Denmark actually produces around 2000 varieties of beer from more than 450 individual breweries. Many smaller companies specialize in traditional brewing techniques.

In Denmark, the beer scene is dominated by Carlsberg. The business traces its origins to the 1700s, to a family farm that almost certainly had its own brewery. The son of the family went to seek his fortune in the big city, and eventually became a brewer there. He was one of the first Danish brewers to use a thermometer. His son Jacob Christian Jacobsen went south to Germany, to Bavaria, to study at the Spaten brewery. It was the moment in Europe when top-fermenting brews (in Denmark, wheat beers) were starting to face challenges from lagers. Carlsberg produced the first bottom-fermented beer commercially made in Denmark – or anywhere in Northern Europe.

Jacob Christian Jacobsen's son Carl also became a brewer. The two men later disagreed to the extent that for a long time each had his own Carlsberg brewery. This historic feud ended shortly before the father's death, and the two breweries merged. The company produces both Carlsberg and Tuborg mainstream lagers, as well as a range of other lagers, notably including the famous Special Brew.

Traditional brewing's decline and the rise of microbreweries has led newcomers to establish a trade organization that will better represent their interests, rather than rely on Bryggeriforeningen, the existing trade body. Danske Bryghuse was officially founded on 21 October 2003.

Left: The Carlsberg brewery in Copenhagen is now the seventh-largest brewery in the world, and has been in operation since 1847. The copper kettles are used to cook the mash at a steady temperature.

STATISTICS

Total production: 8,351,000 hectolitres (220,610,000 gallons) per year

Consumption per capita: 99 litres (26 gallons) per year

Famous breweries: Albani; Brøckhouse; Carlsberg; Ceres; Faxe Bryggeri; Harboe; Tuborg

Famous brands: Bjørne Beer; Carlsberg Elephant; Ceres Red Erik; Faxe Premium; Giraf Classic; Grøn Tuborg

Above: Carlsberg and Tivoli workers take a break from loading duties in July 1952 to enjoy an early morning beer – 9 a.m. to be precise!

Albani Giraf Classic

In 1962 the people of Odense in Denmark were shocked by the news that Kalle the giraffe, a resident of the local zoo, had been found dead in his pen.

The local Albani brewery had used Kalle's image in its advertising and so in his honour it launched a new beer to fund a replacement giraffe for the zoo. Thus Giraf beer was born, and in 1997 a separate brewery was established dedicated to the production of Giraf beers. The range now includes three regular beers – Gold, Strong and Classic. The history of Albani brewery stretches back much further. It was founded in Odense in 1859 and was one of the town's first industrial businesses. Local author Hans Christian Andersen once wrote of Albani beer: 'I cannot praise this beer enough. It is refreshing, tasty and strong. Try it!'

SPECIFICATIONS
Brewery: Albani Briggerierne
Location: Odense
Style: Lager
Colour: Pale golden yellow

Alcohol: 4.6%
Serving temperature: 7°–8°C (44.6°–46.4°F)
Food: Mild-flavoured cheeses, white meats

Brøckhouse Juleøl

This strong seasonal ale from the microbrewery Brøckhouse pours a murky dark brown colour with a very satisfying and lingering tan head. It has an excellent aroma of dark malts, dark chocolate, Christmas spices, caramel and brown sugar, with a hint of cherries.

The flavour is rich and malty with a deep warmth and distinct hints of spices and dark chocolate. The hops provide a fine tangy undertone that nicely balances the sweetness in the finish. This is an excellent beer, and is certainly one of the best seasonal brews to be found anywhere. The brewery itself grew from the dreams of Allan Poulsen, who began as a home brewer, then quit his job in the computing profession in 2002 to start the now successful Brøckhouse brewery.

SPECIFICATIONS
Brewery: Brøckhouse
Location: Hillerød
Style: Belgian strong ale
Colour: Dark brown

Alcohol: 8.3%
Serving temperature: 12°C (50°F)
Food: Traditional Christmas meats and savouries

Grøn Tuborg

One of Europe's most popular beers, Grøn Tuborg pours a clear pale yellow with a large creamy head (which sadly fades too quickly) and a visually pleasing bubble effect. The aroma is sweetcorn and yeast, and remains pleasant as long as the lager is cool. The alcohol can sometimes come through overpoweringly.

Grøn Tuborg was Denmark's first pilsener-type lager. It comes both bottled and canned, but the bottled version is far superior, the other having a rather tinny taste that tends to spoil the overall effect. No matter what one thinks of the flavour, there is no denying that Tuborg is an extremely refreshing drink, a fact that makes it very popular on summer outings. The Tuborg brewery was founded in 1873, and the emphasis was on pilsener in its early years. Today Tuborg is part of the massive Carlsberg organization, Denmark's largest brewery.

SPECIFICATIONS
Brewery: Carlsberg
Location: Copenhagen
Style: Pilsener
Colour: Pale Yellow

Alcohol: 4.6%
Serving temperature: 6°–8°C (43°–46°F)
Food: Fish, chicken, snacks

Carlsberg Elephant

The elephant is the symbol of the largest brewery in Denmark, Carlsberg, which was founded in 1847 by Jacob Christian Jacobsen.

He derived the name of the brewery from a combination of the name of his five-year-old son Carl and the brewery's hillside location (*berg* being Danish for 'hill'). Jacobson was keen on the scientific aspects of brewing, and it was at his laboratories that the first single-cell lager yeast was developed in 1883, which gave brewers greater control over the fermentation process. The brewery is now owned by Kronenbourg and produces a wide range of beers, its best known being its classic pilsener-style golden lager. Carlsberg Elephant is a strong lager in the style of a German bock, with a slightly darker colour and a fairly sweet flavour complemented by malt and hops bitterness.

SPECIFICATIONS
Brewery: Carlsberg
Location: Copenhagen
Style: Lager
Colour: Rich golden yellow

Alcohol: 7.2%
Serving temperature: 8°–10°C (46.4°–50°F)
Food: Fried fish

Ceres Red Erik

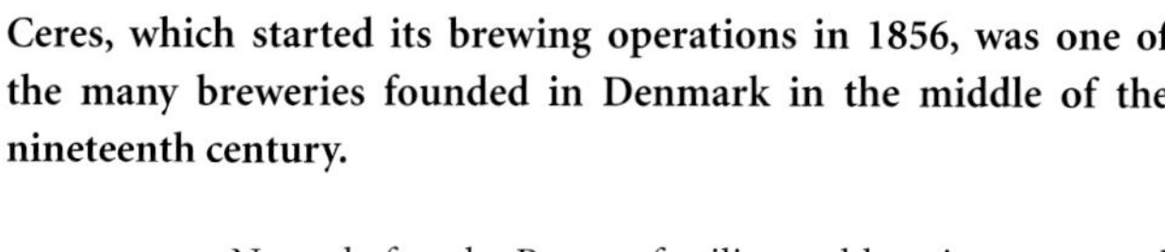

Ceres, which started its brewing operations in 1856, was one of the many breweries founded in Denmark in the middle of the nineteenth century.

Named after the Roman fertility goddess, it was created by a local distiller called M.C. Lottrup, in cooperation with two local chemists called N.S. Aagaard and Knud Redelien – although the latter pair withdrew from the business after a year. The brewery's Red Erik beer, named after the Viking who discovered Greenland and reputedly began brewing there, gets its distinctive colour from the addition of the juices of various fruits and berries. It is a full-bodied strong beer with a refreshingly sharp and slightly sweet flavour.

SPECIFICATIONS

Brewery: Ceres
Location: Aarhus, East Jutland
Style: Fruit beer
Colour: Ruby red
Alcohol: 6.5%
Serving temperature: 7°–8°C (44.6°–46.4°F)
Food: Fruit-based desserts

Thisted Thy Classic

This is a relatively new release from Thisted Bryghus, a small brewery located in the town of Thisted in northwest Jutland. The beer pours dark amber with a rich head, leaving an attractive lacy effect on the glass.

Thy Classic is very full-bodied, which is not surprising, as no fewer than four different malts are used in the brewing process. It has a sharp bitterness characteristic of most Thisted beers, and this lingers for a long time. The Thisted brewery supplies the local area with its beers, which are mostly in the typical Danish pilsener style, but it has recently achieved some national and international acclaim through bottled brews such as Thy Classic. Some of its best are stout- and porter-type ales such as Limfjords Porter.

SPECIFICATIONS

Brewery: Thisted Bryghus
Location: Thisted
Style: Premium lager
Colour: Deep amber
Alcohol: 4.6%
Serving temperature: 8°C (46°F)
Food: Salads, seafood, bread and cheese

Faxe Premium

Faxe is today part of the giant Danish Brewery group, and most of its beers are exported to Germany and other countries, but it started life in 1901 on a very small scale in the scullery of Nikoline and Conrad Neilsen at their house in the small town of Faxe.

The brewery quickly established a widespread reputation for quality beers and, following Conrad's untimely death in 1914, the business was continued by Nikoline. It was renamed the Faxe Bryggeri in 1928. In the 1960s, Bent Bryde-Neilsen, Nikoline's granddaughter, developed Faxe into one of Denmark's largest breweries, establishing export markets in Germany and Sweden. Outside of Denmark, Faxe is best known for Faxe Premium, an all-malt lager with a delicate hop aroma and flavour.

SPECIFICATIONS
Brewery: Faxe Bryggeri
Location: Faxe
Style: Lager
Colour: Golden yellow
Alcohol: 5.5%

Serving temperature: 8°–10°C (46.4°–50°F)
Food: Rich pasta dishes

Bjørne Beer

Outside Denmark, Harboe's Bjørne Beer is very commonly known by the literal translation of its name, Bear Beer, and a polar bear is depicted on the beer's label.

Bjørne Beer has a fragrant herbal hop aroma with background bready malt notes, while the flavour is characterized by a gentle hop bitterness. Launched in 1974, it earned a name for its high alcohol content; the name Bjørne is now applied to a range of different-strength beers, each with different-coloured labels (the strongest have black labels). The Harboe brewery was founded in Skaelskør in 1883 by three local businessmen.

SPECIFICATIONS
Brewery: Harboe
Location: Skaelskør
Style: Strong golden lager
Colour: Deep golden yellow
Alcohol: 8.3%

Serving temperature: 8°–10°C (46.4°–50°F)
Food: Spicy pizzas and pasta dishes

Irish Beers

For many outside Ireland, the perception of Irish brewing begins and ends with one beer style – stout – and what's more, with one particular name, that of Dublin brewer Arthur Guinness. In fact brewing in Ireland dates back at least to the fifth century, when St Patrick arrived in Ireland, reputedly bringing his own brewer with him.

As in other countries, it was the monasteries that established the tradition of ale brewing, although even before then the native Irish drank a barley-based liquor called *courmi.* But Guinness is by far the biggest name in Irish brewing. The firm was established in 1759 as a brewer of traditional amber ales. Around this time, the dark English beer known as porter, named after the London market porters who were its main consumers, was being imported to Ireland in vast quantities. It was not long before Arthur Guinness and other brewers such as Beamish & Crawford came up with their own versions.

The first Guinness porter came out of the St James's Gate brewery in the 1770s, but it was not until 1799 that Arthur Guinness switched to brewing exclusively porter. In 1820, his son, also called Arthur, created a new style of porter that he called extra stout porter, later shortened to stout. This is the famous Guinness Extra Stout.

Still, Guinness does have major rivals such as Heineken Ireland, which incorporates Murphy's, and dynamic young competitors such as the Carlow Brewing Company.

Left: Ireland is famed for its traditional drinking establishments, but the image can mask the fact that Ireland is a major global competitor on the beer market, particularly through its most famous brand, Guinness. A full one million litres of its three million litres annual beer production is exported, and the fan base for its dark ales and porters grows constantly.

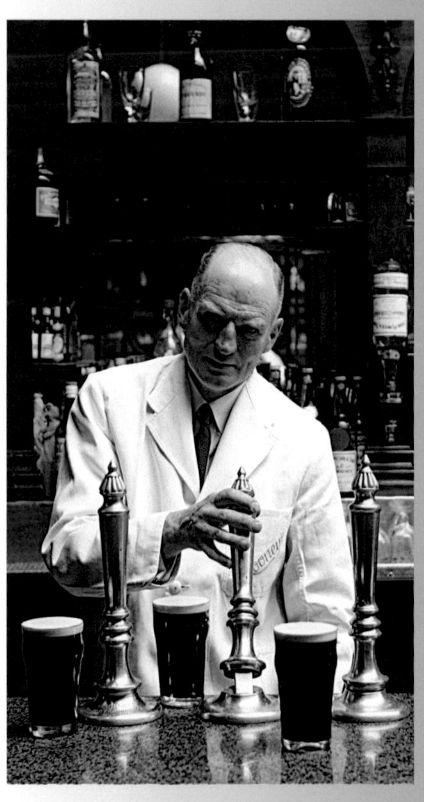

Above: The Guinness brand is rightly famous the world over, and more than any other drink is identified with Ireland. Although Guinness does dominate Irish brewing, the country is also home to a range of other breweries which produce beers of altogether different character.

STATISTICS

Total production: 8,023,000 hectolitres (211,945,000 gallons) per year

Consumption per capita: 125 litres (33 gallons) per year

Famous breweries: Diageo; Murphy Heineken Brewery Ireland Ltd

Famous brands: Guinness Extra Stout; Harp Lager; Kilkenny Irish Beer; Murphy's Irish Red

Guinness Original

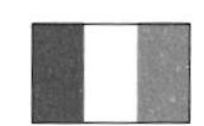

Of the various versions of Guinness currently available, this is the one that comes closest to the original Irish extra stout porter that was created by Arthur Guinness in 1820.

The style quickly caught on, and the original Guinness Extra Stout was soon being exported around the world. This classic style is the beer that made the company's name and will for ever be associated slogans such as 'Guinness is good for you'. Its roasted malts give a distinctive dry, oaky flavour full of toasted malt bitterness. Note that in the United Kingdom this classic dry Irish stout is marketed as Guinness Original, while in the United States Guinness Extra Stout is the name given to a stronger 'export' version of the beer, brewed to 8% alcohol.

SPECIFICATIONS

Brewery: Diageo
Location: Dublin
Style: Dry Irish stout
Colour: Dark red-black
Alcohol: 4.3%
Serving temperature: 12°C (53.6°F)
Food: Classic accompaniment for oysters

Kilkenny Irish Beer

This traditional Irish red ale was originally brewed in 1985, for export only, by Smithwick's at the St Francis Abbey Brewery in Kilkenny (which has been owned by Guinness since 1965).

The ale's sweet, predominantly malty aroma gives way to a smooth, dry and nutty flavour on the palate, with a short, bitter, hoppy finish. Smithwick's is one of the oldest names in Irish brewing, and has been producing ales on the Kilkenny site since 1710, although the Franciscan friars who founded the abbey in the mid-thirteenth century would undoubtedly have been brewers themselves, in the tradition of many monasteries of the time.

SPECIFICATIONS

Brewery: Diageo
Location: Kilkenny
Style: Irish red ale
Colour: Amber-red
Alcohol: 5%
Serving temperature: 9°–10°C (48.2°–50°F)
Food: Boiled bacon and cabbage

Harp Lager

Harp is Ireland's premier lager, its distinctive, refreshing taste having earned it six gold medals in the annual Monde Selection beer tasting contest.

Harp is brewed using golden barley and the choicest hops to give a smooth satisfying lager taste. In blind taste tests in Ireland, Harp receives most favoured status time after time. Since its launch in 1960, Harp has remained a premium Irish lager. In 1996, its already successful export brew was launched in Irish off-licences. Harp 5% Export is a premium lager with a 5% alcohol content and a rich, smooth taste. Harp is also exported to Europe and Canada. In 1997 the brand was renamed Harp Irish Lager in some markets, and is now brewed in the UK as well as Ireland.

SPECIFICATIONS
Brewery: Diageo
Location: Dundalk
Style: Lager
Colour: Pale gold
Alcohol: 5%
Serving temperature: 6°–8°C (43°–46°F)
Food: Seafood, salad, bread and cheese

Murphy's Irish Red

Murphy's Irish Red is brewed to an original recipe that dates back to 1856. It pours a deep burnished bronze with a frothy ivory-coloured head and has a lightly toasted aroma of caramel malts.

On the palate, light carbonation gives it a lively mouthfeel; the flavour is dry with a pronounced hoppy bitterness balanced against grainy malt sweetness. A refreshingly bitter citrus-hop finish helps this beer go down well. The better known Murphy's Irish Stout has a sweeter and milder flavour than either of its main rivals, Guinness Draught and Beamish Stout, but shares the characteristic smooth, creamy texture, pitch-black colour and thick, creamy head. Both were originally brewed by James J. Murphy at the Murphy Brewery in the city of Cork in the southwestern Ireland.

SPECIFICATIONS
Brewery: Murphy Heineken Brewery Ireland Ltd
Location: Cork
Style: Irish red ale
Colour: Clear red-bronze
Alcohol: 5%
Serving temperature: 8°C (46.4°F)
Food: Roast pork

HOLSTEN
A.GUINNESS

Scottish Beers

Although Scotland has a considerably smaller population than its neighbour to the south, it has just as strong a tradition for brewing, which it has always carried out in its own unique way. Scottish beers are traditionally named according to the nineteenth-century shilling system, which relates to the price charged for a hogshead barrel.

Simply put, the stronger the beer, the more expensive it was, so a 40/- (40-shilling) ale would be a very light beer, while the strongest beers would be rated at 80/- (80 shillings) or higher. The terms 'light', 'heavy' and 'export' are commonly used; the strongest barley wines are also known as Scotch ales or Wee Heavies.

The character of brewing in Scotland is partly determined by the climate. As in England, barley flourishes, but the cold, wet conditions that prevail in Scotland mean that the barley grown there is better suited to the production of whisky. The climate also prevents successful growing of hops, so the Scots have always used a variety of alternative bittering agents in their beers, such as ginger, pepper, spices and herbs. Oats flourish in Scottish conditions, and oatmeal has often been used as an ingredient, along with barley, particularly in stout.

Although beer has often played second fiddle to whisky, it has always been extremely popular in Scotland. Still, by the 1970s, there were just two brewers left in Edinburgh – Scottish & Newcastle and Tennent's. In recent years, smaller independent breweries such as Caledonian have managed to gain a foothold in the market.

Left: Scottish beer production has become steadily more prolific over recent years. The beers range from standard high-street lagers such as Tennent's through to very individual brands such as Belhaven 80/- and Orkney Dragonhead Stout. Scotland is gradually building a solid reputation for beer production.

Above: Scotland's reputation when it comes to the production of alcoholic beverages rests mainly on whisky, but beer production is currently undergoing something of a renaissance, as smaller brewers return to traditional brewing methods.

STATISTICS

Total production: 20,000,000 hectolitres (528,344,000 gallons) per year

Consumption per capita: 97 litres (26 gallons) per year

Famous breweries: Belhaven Brewer Company Ltd; Broughton Ales Ltd; Caledonian Brewery; Tennent Caledonian Breweries (Interbrew)

Famous brands: Belhaven 80 Shilling; Caledonian 80 Shilling; Orkney Dragonhead Stout; Tennent's Lager

Belhaven 80 Shilling

Based in the town of Dunbar, 48 km (30 miles) from Edinburgh, Belhaven is one of Scotland's largest regional brewers. It is also one of the oldest, with a history stretching back at least 300 years.

The first known documents confirming the existence of the brewery date from 1719, when the brewery was bought by John Johnstone. It is believed to be much older, as the present brewery stands on the site of a former Benedictine monastery built in the twelfth century. Belhaven 80 Shilling was once described by the Austrian Emperor as 'the Burgundy of Scotland', and Dr Johnson's biographer James Boswell was also known to be a fan. It has a rich red-hued colour and a deeply complex, malt-led flavour, with sweet caramel, dark fruit and nutty roasted malt notes.

SPECIFICATIONS

Brewery: Belhaven
Location: Dunbar, East Lothian
Style: Scottish strong export ale
Colour: Dark red-brown
Alcohol: 3.9%
Serving temperature: 10°–13°C (50°–55.4°F)
Food: Spicy Chinese dishes

Caledonian 80 Shilling

Scottish beers are traditionally classified by two systems. The first describes the beers in order of strength from light to heavy, and export to strong. The other method of classification is also based on the alcohol content and the level of tax applied.

Eighty shillings (written as 80/-) was the rate applied to export-strength beers such as this rich, malty red-brown ale. This beer is characterized by a deep fruity aroma with hints of berry fruit and spicy hop background notes, and rich fruity malt flavours balanced by a fragrant hop dryness. Caledonian 80 Shilling was named official beer of the Edinburgh Festival 2004. The Caledonian Brewery was founded in 1869 by George Lorimer Jr, in conjunction with Edinburgh brewer Robert Clarke.

SPECIFICATIONS

Brewery: Caledonian
Location: Edinburgh
Style: Scottish strong export ale
Colour: Rust red-brown
Alcohol: 4.1%
Serving temperature: 10°C (50°F)
Food: Roast beef or game

Orkney Dragonhead Stout

Founded in 1988 by Roger White and his wife, Irene, the multiple award-winning Orkney company is the most northerly brewery in Britain, being situated on the largest of the Isles of Orkney, off the northeastern coast of the Scottish mainland.

The brewery is housed in an old schoolhouse surrounded by two-and-a-half hectares (six acres) of grassland and lakes, and offers in its line-up six regular beers, each of which has a name inspired by the historical association of the islands with the Vikings. Dragonhead Stout is a first-rate example of the style, packed with rich, sweet roasted malt flavours balanced with an astringent dry bitterness provided by a complex blend of hops.

SPECIFICATIONS
Brewery: Orkney
Location: Sandwick, Isles of Orkney
Style: Stout
Colour: Black
Alcohol: 4%
Serving temperature: 8°–10°C (46°–50°F)
Food: Strong cheeses

Tennent's Lager

Tennent's Wellpark brewery in the centre of Glasgow, close to the cathedral, has been in continuous operation since 1885, although beer is known to have been brewed on the site since 1556, making this one of the oldest brewing locations in Britain.

The company was the first brewery in the United Kingdom to produce a lager, which it launched in 1924. It remains a distinctive brew with a clean, crisp, well-balanced taste combining sweet malty flavours with a refreshingly tangy hop bitterness. The brewery is now owned by the Belgian global giant Interbrew.

SPECIFICATIONS
Brewery: Tennent Caledonian
Location: Glasgow
Style: Lager
Colour: Golden yellow
Alcohol: 5%
Serving temperature: 6°–8°C (43°–46°F)
Food: Hot spicy curries

English Beers

Brewing and drinking beer have always been a key part of the English life. Even the wine-drinking Normans could not replace beer with their favourite tipple in the eleventh century, and the Domesday Book records evidence of a thriving commercial brewing industry.

Although the English enjoy a long tradition of small-scale domestic brewing, the monasteries were by far the largest producers of beer until their dissolution in the sixteenth century. Their practices remain an influence on brewing to this day, with methods such as the Burton Union used by Marston's having their origins in medieval monastic brewing techniques. The English have a reputation around the world as lovers of warm, flat beer, but most English ales are best served at cellar temperature, while some of the stronger, fuller-flavoured beers are best served like red wine at slightly below room temperature.

English beers come in a wide variety of styles. In the first half of the twentieth century, mild was by far the most popular, quaffed in large quantities by workers. Brewed with fewer hops than bitters and pale ales, mild beer is named for its flavour rather than its alcohol content, and comes in a range of strengths. From the 1950s onwards, bitter became more popular, but by the 1960s traditional cask ales were threatened with extinction due to the increasing trend towards keg beer production. These are pasteurized and filtered to ensure consistency and increase keeping quality, but lack the character of 'real' ale.

Despite the continued dominance of a small handful of global brewers, who produce more than 80% of beer consumed in the United Kingdom, this trend has been partly reversed by the work of Camra, the Campaign for Real Ale, which fights for the values supported by small brewers using traditional methods.

Left: Despite recent rationalization and the demise of many small independent breweries, England is blessed with a bewildering array of quality distinctive beers. The traditional British pint glass can be filled with such individual brews as Badger Tanglefoot.

Above: England possesses an unusually high density of public houses stretched throughout its towns, cities and villages. Many feature 'guest' or speciality beers that promote a broader palate among the drinking public.

STATISTICS

Total production: 40,000,000 hectolitres (1,056,689,000 gallons) per year

Consumption per capita: 97 litres (26 gallons) per year

Famous breweries: Fuller's, George Gale & Co.; Greene King; Marston's; Scottish & Newcastle; Theakston's

Famous brands: Badger Tanglefoot; Bass Pale Ale; Fuller's 1845; Gale's Trafalgar; Marston's Pedigree; Newcastle Brown Ale; Old Speckled Hen; Theakston's Old Peculier

Badger Tanglefoot

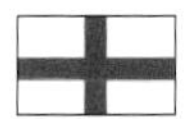

According to legend, Tanglefoot acquired its name when the head brewer tripped over his own feet after having sampled several tankards of this strong but 'deceptively drinkable' ale.

It is a robustly flavoured beer, full of hoppy bitterness that dominates the fruity yeast and malt flavours on the palate, and its extremely dry, lemon-scented bitter finish is due to the use of Challenger hops. Badger is the trading name of the Hall & Woodhouse brewery, founded in 1777 by Charles Hall as the Ansty Brewery. It became Hall & Woodhouse when Charles's son joined forces with George Woodhouse, and the brewery moved to its present site in Blandford St Mary in 1899. The badger is a common animal locally and was adopted as the brewery's emblem.

SPECIFICATIONS
Brewery: Badger (Hall & Woodhouse Ltd)
Location: Blandford St Mary, Dorset
Style: Strong pale ale
Colour: Pale golden straw
Alcohol: 5%
Serving temperature: 12°C (53.6°F)
Food: Grilled red meats, such as lamb chops

Black Sheep Ale

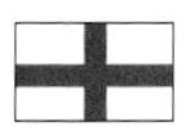

Black Sheep Ale is a full-flavoured premium bitter, with a rich fruity aroma. It is brewed with many generous handfuls of rich Golding hops, giving a bittersweet malty taste, followed by a long, dry and bitter finish.

The Black Sheep brewery was the creation of Paul Theakston, whose family have been brewers of fine ales in the little town of Masham, North Yorkshire, for generations. In 1992, some five years after the brewery was absorbed by the Scottish and Newcastle group, Paul decided to re-establish his independence by setting up a new yet traditional family brewery, and Black Sheep Ale began to appear in pubs in and around the Yorkshire Dales. The beer is one of the most popular to be found in the region.

SPECIFICATIONS
Brewery: Black Sheep Brewery
Location: Masham, N. Yorks.
Style: Traditional ale
Colour: Amber
Alcohol: 4.4%
Serving temperature: 10°C (50°F)
Food: Meat pies, roasts

Charles Wells Bombardier

A classic English best bitter, Bombardier is strong and full of flavour and character, yet not at all heavy, making it a surprisingly easy beer to drink.

It has a fruity flavour, reminiscent of raisins and sultanas, and a lingering, dry, subtle bitterness that comes from the use of Challenger hops; while crystal malt and Goldings hops help to produce its distinctive pale copper colour. The self-styled 'Patron pint of England' is now closely associated with St George's Day, following an intensive marketing campaign by the brewery. In tune with its patriotic values, Bombardier Premium Bitter is available in imperial pint measure (568ml) bottles. Established in 1876, Charles Wells is one of England's largest independent regional brewers, and is still run by descendants of the founder, based at the Eagle Brewery in Bedford.

SPECIFICATIONS
Brewery: Charles Wells
Location: Bedford, Bedfordshire
Style: Best bitter
Colour: Dark red-brown
Alcohol: 5.5%
Serving temperature: 12°C (53.6°F)
Food: Traditional English battered fish and chips

Fuller's 1845

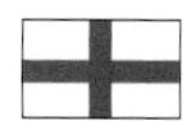

Records show that brewing has taken place on the present site of the Fuller's brewery for at least 325 years, though Fuller, Smith and Turner was founded only in 1845. This strong traditional ale was launched in 1995 to celebrate the brewery's 150th anniversary; Prince Charles added the hops to the first batch brewed.

After primary fermentation, the beer spends two weeks in conditioning tanks before it is filtered, then re-seeded with fresh yeast and bottled. The bottles are then allowed to condition for two weeks. It has a lively, yeasty, malty aroma with an orange fruit character. On the palate it is smooth and full-bodied, with a mouthfeel almost like that of drinking a liqueur. A powerful toasty, fruity maltiness with hints of raisins, chocolate and toffee overwhelms the taste buds at first, but is soon countered by a dry, hop bitterness that lingers to a well-balanced finish.

SPECIFICATIONS
Brewery: Fuller, Smith & Turner plc
Location: Chiswick, London
Style: Strong ale
Colour: Red-brown
Alcohol: 6.3%
Serving temperature: 13°C (55.4°F)
Food: Richly flavoured stews

Gale's Trafalgar

This powerful seasonal ale is brewed in the autumn every year to commemorate Trafalgar Day, 21 October, which marks Nelson's victory against Napoleon and the combined French and Spanish forces at the naval Battle of Trafalgar in 1805.

Accordingly, Gale's Trafalgar is brewed using only ingredients that were available in Nelson's day – maris otter pale malt and crystal malt, and Challenger and Fuggles hops. The aroma is surprisingly delicate for a beer of this strength, with subtle notes of fruity malt and hops, while the flavour is sweet, spicy, fruity and malty with a good balance of hop bitterness. The cask version of Trafalgar is brewed to approximately half the alcohol strength. In 2005, a new beer called Trafalgar 200 appeared, which was brewed in the cask to celebrate the 200th anniversary of Nelson's victory.

SPECIFICATIONS
Brewery: George Gale & Co.
Location: Horndean, Hampshire
Style: Strong ale
Colour: Dark ruby red
Alcohol: 9%
Serving temperature: 13°–14°C (55.4°–57.2°F)
Food: Dark meat and game dishes

Greene King Abbot Ale

Abbot Ale, first brewed in 1955, has become firmly established as Greene King's flagship brand.

It benefits from a long secondary fermentation at relatively high temperatures, which ensures a full-flavoured beer with rich fruity malts on the palate. Two varieties of hops are used to give an appetizing bitterness in a long, dry finish and perfumed floral aromas. The beer's name reflects the long tradition of brewing in this ancient town – the Domesday Book shows that brewing was already taking place at the great abbey of St Edmundsbury as early as AD 1086, and the water used by the brewery today is drawn from the same chalk beds as used by the monks for their beers.

SPECIFICATIONS
Brewery: Greene King
Location: Bury St Edmunds, Suffolk
Style: Pale ale
Colour: Deep amber
Alcohol: 5.0%
Serving temperature: 10°–13°C (50°–55.4°F)
Food: Roast red meats

Morland Old Speckled Hen

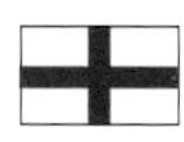

Old Speckled Hen was originally produced by the Morland brewery of Abingdon in Oxfordshire, which was founded in 1711. In 1998, Morland acquired the ailing Ruddles brewery of Oakham in Leicestershire, which soon after met its own demise and in 1999 was taken over by the Suffolk brewer Greene King.

Greene King adopted Old Speckled Hen along with Ruddles County. Old Speckled Hen is a warming and very full-bodied beer. Rich, plummy aromas are laden with intense malty sweetness, while on the palate malt loaf and toffee flavours give a sweetness that is balanced by a long, dry and satisfying bitter finish. The inspiration for the beer's name, rather than being a fowl, was actually a much-loved old canvas-covered saloon car – the 'awld speckled 'un' – that over the years had become speckled in paint.

SPECIFICATIONS
Brewery: Greene King
Location: Bury St Edmunds, Suffolk
Style: Pale ale
Colour: Deep golden amber
Alcohol: 5.2%
Serving temperature: 11°–13°C (51.8°–55.4°F)
Food: Cooked cured ham

Bass Pale Ale

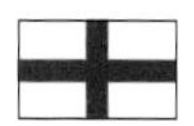

This most famous of British ales has been brewed in Burton upon Trent since 1777. Its iconic red triangle, which adorns Bass labels to this day, became the first registered trademark in Britain in 1875.

Bass Pale Ale remains inextricably linked to its home town of Burton upon Trent due to the unique mineral properties of the local water, which gives Bass beers their characteristic sulphurous aroma – which cannot be replicated successfully anywhere else. Originally brewed to a higher alcohol and hop content to preserve it during its long sea voyage to India, this is an amber-coloured top-fermented beer with a sweet, fruity aroma, caramel and malt on the palate and a dry, bitter hoppy finish.

SPECIFICATIONS
Brewery: Marston's
Location: Burton upon Trent, Staffordshire
Style: India pale ale
Colour: Amber red
Alcohol: 5.2%
Serving temperature: 10°C (50°F)
Food: Smoked fish or sausages

Marston's Pedigree Bitter

First brewed in 1834 and still made to the same recipe, using maris otter barley with Fuggles and Goldings hops and a 150-year-old strain of yeast, Marston's Pedigree is a living reminder of the way beer used to be in the middle of the nineteenth century.

It is brewed using water drawn from one of seven wells on the brewery site and is the only beer in the world that is still made using the Burton Union system, a relic of Victorian brewing that comprises a series of giant oak vats linked by copper tubes to an iron trough. It produces a subtle, complex beer with nutty, malty dryness balanced against sweet, fruity flavours of apples and pears. The Burton Union method also produces excess yeast that is used to start the next batch of beer.

SPECIFICATIONS
Brewery: Marston's
Location: Burton upon Trent, Staffordshire
Style: Pale ale
Colour: Pale amber-red
Alcohol: 4.5%
Serving temperature: 12°C (53.6°F)
Food: Roast beef

Samuel Smith's Organic Lager

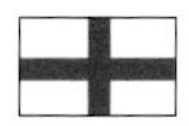

A full-bodied lager with lots of malt and hop character, Sam Smith's Organic is a touch hoppier than many lagers, yet remains perfectly balanced.

Lightly kilned lager malt grown in the UK is the main ingredient, with a substantial addition of organic Vienna malt and organic Hallertau Perle hops from Germany. Another product of this famous old brewery is Samuel Smith's Organic Ale, a delicately flavoured golden ale in which subtle fruity esters from the Samuel Smith yeast strain interact with a background of maltiness and fresh hops. Samuel Smith's organic beers are reminiscent of early twentieth-century brews not only in the brewing process and flavour, but in the label design as well.

SPECIFICATIONS
Brewery: Samuel Smith's
Location: Tadcaster, Yorkshire
Style: Lager
Colour: Pale gold
Alcohol: 5%
Serving temperature: 7–9°C (44–48°F)
Food: Poached salmon, crab, Quiche Lorraine

Newcastle Brown Ale

One of the most popular ales in Britain, Newcastle Brown Ale was launched in 1927 after three years of development by head brewer Jim Porter. The origins of the Newcastle Breweries stretch back to 1770, when John Barras & Co. founded the Gateshead Brewery.

In 1890, John Barras moved across the river Tyne and formed Newcastle Breweries Ltd. The brew was an immediate success, winning several gold medals at the International Brewers' Exhibition in London in 1928. These medals were incorporated into the bottle's label, along with the blue star logo adopted as the company trade mark in 1913. Still brewed to the original recipe, the ale has a dry, nutty flavour with a delicate floral aroma.

SPECIFICATIONS
Brewery: Scottish & Newcastle
Location: Newcastle-upon-Tyne, Tyne & Wear
Style: Brown ale
Colour: Deep mahogany brown
Alcohol: 4.7%
Serving temperature: 10ºC (50ºF)
Food: Sausages and mash

Theakston Old Peculier

Old Peculier was the beer that made Theakston's brewery in the North Yorkshire town of Masham famous, and left many an unwary soldier in nearby Catterick Garrison with a thick head.

A rich, dark, smooth-tasting beer with a unique and unequalled flavour, it has a large and enthusiastic following all over Britain and around the world. If you want to find out what an old ale tastes like, Old Peculier is a great example. It is a must try for anyone in the mood for something different and should not be too demanding of even the most middle of the road drinker, although its strength should not be underestimated! The Theakston brewery was established as a brewpub in 1827, with the current brewery dating from the 1870s.

SPECIFICATIONS
Brewery: Theakston
Location: Masham, N. Yorks.
Style: Old ale
Colour: Dark brown
Alcohol: 5.6%
Serving temperature: 10ºC (50ºF)
Food: Rib of beef

ARENAL
BAR
EL Pescaito Frito
FRIED FISH
COMIDAS
CASERAS
HAY MENÚ
21
7UP
DE
PESCADO

Spanish Beers

Spain has experienced a decline in the variety of beers produced over recent decades, mainly through the closing of many of its microbreweries. The country still produces a range of quality beers, however, either through its eight major beers producers or through some of the independent breweries still managing to make a living.

The historian Pliny mentions the use of beer in Spain under the names of *celia* and *ceria*, and in Gaul under that of *cerevisia*; and remarks that: 'The natives who inhabit the west of Europe have a liquid with which they intoxicate themselves, made from corn and water. The manner of making this liquid is somewhat different in Gaul, Spain and other countries, and it is called by different names, but its nature and properties are everywhere the same. The people in Spain in particular brew this liquid so well that it will keep good a long time. So exquisite is the cunning of mankind in gratifying their vicious appetites that they have thus invented a method to make water itself produce intoxication.'

The quality of Spanish beer in the sixteenth century was apparently poor; when Charles V – who liked a tipple or two – became king, he immediately passed a law ensuring that all beer was pure. Today, Spain has nine large breweries, the oldest of which is Damm SA of Barcelona, established in 1876. Many microbreweries have closed in recent years, and most larger concerns specialize in brewing foreign beers under licence. There are still good-quality indigenous beers, however, such as Alhambra, Cruzcampo, Estrella Damm and San Miguel.

Left: Tapas bars such as the one shown left in Seville, southern Spain, are a popular location for Spaniards to relax and enjoy a beer with a small snack or two. The high temperatures in Spain have encouraged lighter beers to flourish in the country, despite competition from other traditional Spanish drinks such as sherry and wine.

Above : Beer is a refreshing accompaniment to the traditional Spanish tapas, particularly on a hot summer's day.

STATISTICS

Total production: 30,671,000 hectolitres (810,242,000 gallons) per year

Consumption per capita: 75 litres (20 gallons) per year

Famous breweries: Damm; Grupo Cruzcampo; San Miguel

Famous brands: Cruzcampo; Estrella Damm; Voll-Damm; San Miguel 1516

Cruzcampo

Cruzcampo is the flagship beer of Spain's largest brewing group. It has a light, dry hop character with slightly sour citrus notes balanced by a gently sweet, grainy maltiness.

The Cruzcampo brewery group was formed through the merger in 1987 of a number of smaller regional breweries, although Cruzcampo beer has a history stretching back 100 years to 1904. The brewery currently operates across five sites in the Andalucia region, with its headquarters in Seville. The group was taken over by Guinness in 1991, then again a few years later by Heineken, which merged it with El Aguila of Madrid.

SPECIFICATIONS

Brewery: Grupo Cruzcampo
Location: Seville, Andalucia
Style: Lager
Colour: Deep yellow-orange
Alcohol: 5%
Serving temperature: 6°–8°C (42.8°–46.4°F)
Food: Cured dried meats and sausages

Estrella Damm

Damm makes the most popular beers in the Catalonia region of northern Spain, and Estrella Damm is its flagship brand.

It is a smooth, easy-drinking pale lager with a creamy head, a touch of floral hops in the aroma and a clean, dry flavour with a slightly bitter hop finish. The brewery has its headquarters in Barcelona; it was founded in 1876 by Auguste Kuentzmann Damm, a native of France's Alsace. Today the company has an extensive network of brewing plants across Spain. Damm was the first brewer in Spain to produce the bottom-fermented golden beers that were becoming popular towards the end of the nineteenth century.

SPECIFICATIONS

Brewery: Damm
Location: Barcelona, Catalonia
Style: Lager
Colour: Blonde
Alcohol: 5.4%
Serving temperature: 5°–7°C (41°–44.6°F)
Food: Cold cooked meats and ham

Voll-Damm

Voll-Damm is a strong pale lager in the Dortmunder style, with a full body, a deep golden colour and a rich, fruity malt flavour which is reminiscent of grapes and plums.

The beer epitomizes the German roots of the company, and Voll-Damm is now one of the largest brewers in Spain, with a growing export business. Most of the brewing takes place at the La Bohemia brewery in Barcelona, close to the famous Sagrada Familia, while malting is carried out at La Moravia malthouse. Damm has a close association with Barcelona's cultural and sporting life, and was a sponsor for the 1982 Football World Cup and the Olympic Games in 1992. This is one of its strongest beers, its 7.2% abv making it a serious tipple.

SPECIFICATIONS
Brewery: Damm
Location: Barcelona, Catalonia
Style: Strong lager
Colour: Deep golden yellow
Alcohol: 7.2%
Serving temperature: 8°C (46.4°F)
Food: Smoked fish

San Miguel 1516

San Miguel 1516 is a smooth, easy-drinking pale golden lager with malty cereal aromas with overtones of hops, honey, citrus fruit and apples.

On the palate, it has a slightly sweet malty character balanced by moderate hop bitterness. The name 1516 refers to the year the Spanish king Carlos V first invited German brewers to come to Spain to introduce their craft to a predominantly wine-drinking nation. Despite the Spanish name, the company is actually a branch of San Miguel in the Philippines, which has been brewing in Manila since 1890. It entered the Spanish market in 1946, and has become the leading beer brand in Spain.

SPECIFICATIONS
Brewery: San Miguel
Location: Lerida, Catalonia
Style: Lager
Colour: Pale golden yellow
Alcohol: 5.4%
Serving temperature: 6°–8°C (42.8°–46.4°F)
Food: A rich fish stew

French Beers

Wine is such a dominant influence on French culture that it is hard to imagine that the French have ever drunk anything else. Yet ancient Gaul was a land of brewers. It was only after the Roman invasion and their subsequent influence that wine became prevalent. Even then, northern France remained a centre of brewing excellence.

Today, beer is drunk widely throughout the country, although it is treated principally as a thirst-quencher and receives none of the reverence shown by the French towards wine. The majority of France's breweries are located in the Alsace region and north of Paris. The pervasive German influence found here means that most French beers are versions of German lagers and tend to be light, uncomplicated and refreshing.

France's largest brewer is Strasbourg-based Kronenbourg, a company with a proud history dating back to 1664. In 1970, Kronenbourg was acquired by the BSN group. BSN later became Danone, which in 2002 sold out to the British multinational Scottish & Newcastle, now one of Europe's largest brewing groups. The next-biggest player is Dutch giant Heineken, which has several significant brands, including Pelforth.

Besides Alsace, the other area of consequence in French brewing is the Nord-Pas-de-Calais region, centred on the city of Lille, close to the Belgian border. The distinctive local style here is *bière de garde*, a strong, top-fermented ale traditionally made in farmhouses and stored for drinking in summer. The style is leading a revival in brewing's popularity across France.

Left: French brewing has, as in most other countries, its dominant major player; that role belongs to the Brasseries Kronenbourg, under the ownership of the huge Scottish & Newcastle group. Kronenbourg 1664 lager is a worldwide bestseller, but also an example of how a mass-produced lager can be premium quality.

Above: France's tradition of beer production is a great one, and it has generated some of the most beautiful label artwork.

STATISTICS

Total production: 18,100,000 hectolitres (478,151,000 gallons) per year
Consumption per capita: 36 litres (10 gallons) per year
Famous breweries: Brasserie Castelain; Brasserie Duyck; Brasseries Kronenbourg (Scottish & Newcastle); Fischer (Heineken)
Famous brands: Fischer Tradition; Jade La Bio; Jenlain; Kronenbourg 1664

Ch'ti Triple

Ch'ti means 'native of the region' in the local Picardy dialect. It is an eminently appropriate title for the range of beers Castelain makes at the Brasserie de Bénifontaine, located in a small village just north of Lens with a coal-mining heritage.

These are examples of the traditional local *bière de garde*, brewed using 100% malt, matured for up to eight weeks, and available in several distinct versions. This one takes its name from the Belgian classification 'tripel', which usually designates a top-fermented ale; Castelain's version is bottom-fermented. Its amber-gold colour is reminiscent of aged rum, the aroma is fragrantly floral, while the flavour is fruity, over an underlying dry, nutty bitterness. Other beers in the range include Ch'ti Blonde and Ch'ti Brune.

SPECIFICATIONS
Brewery: Brasserie Castelain
Location: Bénifontaine, Nord-Pas-de-Calais
Style: Bière de garde
Colour: Amber-gold
Alcohol: 7.5%
Serving temperature: 10°–13°C (50°–55.4°F)
Food: Sharp-flavoured fresh cheeses flavoured with herbs

Jade La Bio

The ever-increasing popularity in France of *produits de l'agriculture biologique* (organic produce) applies as much to beer as any other area of food and drink, and some brewers are picking up on this trend in the beers they choose to offer.

This example from the Castelain brewery of Bénifontaine in northern France is one of the market leaders, its organic status indicated by the green 'AB' logo on the label. It is an easy-drinking bottom-fermented lager (like all of Castelain's beers), pale in colour, filtered but not pasteurized, with fresh herbal aromas and a refreshingly hoppy flavour. Jade is available either in a small bottle with a standard metal cap or in a larger Champagne-style bottle with a cork.

SPECIFICATIONS
Brewery: Brasserie Castelain
Location: Bénifontaine, Nord-Pas-de-Calais
Style: Lager
Colour: Pale golden yellow
Alcohol: 4.6%
Serving temperature: 7°–8°C (44.6°–46.4°F)
Food: Simple grilled fish or chicken dishes

Jenlain

The flagship beer of the Duyck brewer is an unpasteurized bottle-conditioned top-fermented ale matured for not less than 40 days.

The aroma is dominated by fruity malt and burnt caramel with hints of spices and grassy hops. It feels smooth, creamy and slightly effervescent in the mouth and has initially sweet, malty, ripe melon flavours that give way to a dry, spicy finish with a light hoppy bite. The brewery also produces a pale version of the beer, Jenlain Blonde; for those after something a bit more exotic, two variants have added flavourings: La J Absinthe has a lightly aniseed flavour, while La J Gingembre (ginger) is subtly spicy with a hint of lemon. Another member of the Duyck family is Torra, inspired by Corsican tradition.

SPECIFICATIONS

Brewery: Brasserie Duyck
Location: Jenlain, Nord-Pas-de-Calais
Style: Bière de garde
Colour: Amber-red
Alcohol: 6.5%
Serving temperature: 6°–8°C (42.8°–46.4°F)
Food: Rich, hearty stews

Fischer Tradition

The flagship beer of Strasbourg's Fischer brewery, Fischer Tradition is a typical Alsace-style blonde lager which is presented in an attractive embossed bottle with a ceramic flip-top lid.

It pours with a thick, creamy head and gives off a light, malty aroma. Moderate carbonation adds a bit of weight to its light body, and the flavour is sweet and refreshingly fruity. Fischer Tradition is also available as an Amber version, and a more recent addition to the range is Pêcheur, an authentically grainy, fruity Pilsner with a crisp, clean flavour. The Fischer brewery was started in 1821, established in Strasbourg by Jean Fischer. In 1996 the brewery became part of Heineken.

SPECIFICATIONS

Brewery: Fischer (Heineken)
Location: Schiltigheim, Alsace
Style: Lager
Colour: Sunny golden yellow
Alcohol: 6%
Serving temperature: 6°C (42.8°F)
Food: Goes well with simple pasta dishes

Kanterbräu

The Kanterbräu brewery produces a cheap but very palatable lager which is highly popular. Kanterbräu, the beer of Maître Kanter, is a traditional lager with just the right amount of bitterness.

The name comes from the eponymous master brewer who founded a number of brasseries in the east of France, back in the 1930s. The brasseries produced their own beer and offered a menu based on traditional Alsatian dishes. The Tavernes de Maître Kanter carry on the same tradition, with over 60 restaurants in the major towns and cities in France, offering simple, hearty Alsatian dishes washed down with wine or beer (although the beer is now bought in directly from the brewery). The beer has a good, white head that is fairly dense and persists for some time.

SPECIFICATIONS
Brewery: Kanterbräu
Location: Strasbourg
Style: Lager
Colour: Pale yellow
Alcohol: 4.5%
Serving temperature: 7°C (44°F)
Food: Picnics, barbecues

Kronenbourg 1664

When a new beer was launched in 1952 to commemorate the coronation of Queen Elizabeth II, Kronenbourg decided to name it after the year in which the young Jérome Hatt was awarded his brewing diploma and set up his first brewery in the centre of Strasbourg.

This strong, traditional lager is given a lengthy period of maturation. It has an aroma of green, leafy hops, malt and floral yeast, with hints of ripe plums, apricots and honey. It is smooth and dense on the palate, full of well-balanced ripe fruit flavours, with a pleasantly bitter, floral, hop finish. Variations in the range include 1664 Brune, a mellow brown ale.

SPECIFICATIONS
Brewery: Brasseries Kronenbourg (Scottish & Newcastle)
Location: Strasbourg, Alsace
Style: Premium lager
Colour: Dark gold
Alcohol: 5.9%
Serving temperature: 9°–10°C (48.2°–50°F)
Food: Serve as an aperitif

Kronenbourg Tourtel

A non-alcoholic beer claiming to have all the qualities of a normal beer, Tourtel is made with pure malt and generously hopped.

It is named after the innovative Tourtel brothers, Jules and Prosper, who owned the brewery in Tantonville, near Nancy, where Louis Pasteur first observed the role of yeast in fermentation. Tourtel has a delicate, grainy, malty, hoppy aroma with hints of lemon and honey. It feels smooth, light and slightly sparkling in the mouth, and the flavour is well balanced between sweetness and bitterness. It is also available in a brown ale version with a thick, creamy head and a rich, sweet and mildly bitter flavour.

SPECIFICATIONS
Brewery: Brasseries Kronenbourg (Scottish & Newcastle)
Location: Strasbourg, Alsace
Style: Low-alcohol lager
Colour: Straw yellow
Alcohol: 0.5%
Serving temperature: 6°C (42.8°F)
Food: Steamed fish or chicken

Pelforth

A brewery which is now part of the Heineken group, Pelforth produced its first beer, a lager called Pelican, in 1914.

In 1935, Jean Deflandre, the son of Armand, succeeded in putting together two malts of barley with an English yeast to create a revolutionary beer. He named it Pelforth 43, Pel for Pelican, fort for strong (the French word *forte* means strong) because it contains a lot of malt, and the h added to give it an English feel. Production ceased during World War II but restarted in 1950. The '43' was abandoned and the ale was now sold in bottles of 25cl, 33cl, and in casks of all sizes. In 1972, the brewery adopted the Pelforth name permanently. In 1986 it was bought by Français de Brasserie, which in turn was acquired by Heineken in 1988. In addition to the Blonde and Brune, a Pelforth Amber was introduced in 2003.

SPECIFICATIONS
Brewery: Pelforth
Location: Mons-en-Baroeul
Style: Brown ale
Colour: Brown
Alcohol: 6.5%
Serving temperature: 10°–12°C (50°–54°F)
Food: Roast rack of lamb

Luxembourg Beers

The Grand Duchy of Luxembourg (originally Lützelburg) was one of the largest fiefs in the Holy Roman Empire. The Grand Duchy may be overshadowed by the international advertising campaigns of its European neighbours' legendary master brewers, but the Luxembourgeois and beer cognoscenti worldwide know better.

As the centuries-old Luxembourg slogan touts, 'Onse Be'er ass gudd.' The Grand Duchy has a very respectable number of breweries, given its tiny size. Of course, the multinationals (in the form of Interbrew) control the lion's share of the market. More than 600,000 hectolitres (158,500 gallons) were brewed each year during the 1970s and 1980s, with a peak of more than 800,000 hectolitres (211,500 gallons) in 1976. Since then, there has been a definite downhill trend. Since the millennium, beer production has dropped below 400,000 hectolitres (106,000 gallons) for the first time since the late 1950s, and it is hard to see how it can ever go much higher again. On a brighter note, new brewpubs, which may be the future of brewing in Luxembourg, have bumped up the brewery numbers. The country, with its population of only 400,000, currently has seven breweries.

As far as styles are concerned, Luxembourg, no doubt influenced by the influx of beers from the east, moved over to bottom fermentation much earlier than Belgium. By 1872, 27 of its 32 breweries had already made the switch to lager. By 1900 the last brewery had given up top fermentation.

The most visible beer brand in Luxembourg is Bofferding. In competition with local rival Mousel, Bofferding has put most of its marketing efforts behind just one beer, a pilsener. The company's 150-year heritage, combined with a very modern factory and an emphasis on freshness, has led to Bofferding Pils becoming the leading national brand.

Left: A bustling scene in the Place D'Armes in the City of Luxembourg. Such venues are great places to sample some of Luxembourg's fine brews, although you may have to choose your bar or restaurant well to avoid commonplace international brands.

STATISTICS

Total production: 375,000 hectolitres(9,900,000 gallons) per year
Consumption per capita: 107 litres(28 gallons) per year
Famous breweries: Bofferding, Luxeumbourg-Mousel-Diekirch, Simon
Famous brands: Mousel, Simon Dinkel

Above: A view of the filtration tanks inside La Brasserie Simon, one of only two independent breweries in Luxembourg. The other brewery is Bofferding.

Bofferding Pils

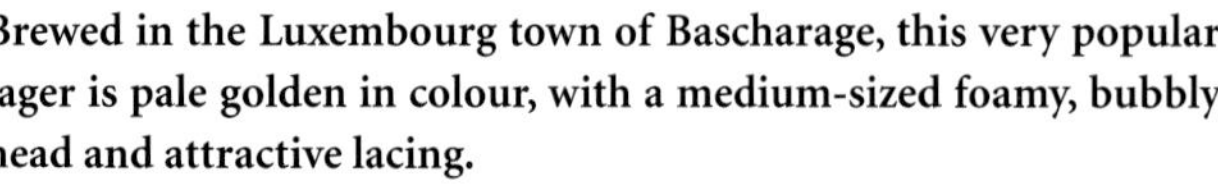

Brewed in the Luxembourg town of Bascharage, this very popular lager is pale golden in colour, with a medium-sized foamy, bubbly head and attractive lacing.

The aroma is malty, but rather weak. There is a strong, sweet hoppy flavour with a big hoppy finish and a bittersweet aftertaste. It is a good, solid pilsener-style beer. The Brasserie Bofferding produces several beer styles, some of which are seasonal. A very popular picturesque tourist resort, Bascharage is located on the main Luxembourg–Paris road and lies at the crossroads of the mining district and the green valleys of the Capellan county.

SPECIFICATIONS
Brewery: Brasserie Bofferding
Location: Bascharage
Style: Lager
Colour: Pale yellow
Alcohol: 5.0%
Serving temperature: 6°–8°C (42°–46°F)
Food: Serve as an apéritif

Premium Diekirch

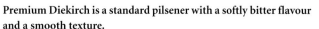

Premium Diekirch is a standard pilsener with a softly bitter flavour and a smooth texture.

It is one of the leading beer brands produced in Luxembourg and was originally brewed by the Diekirch brewery, which was founded in 1871 by the merger of three smaller breweries in the town of the same name. In 1999, Diekirch merged with one of its main rivals, the Mousel brewery of Rheinfelden, and the Mousel brewery was closed down, with production of that brewery's beers being moved to the Diekirch plant. The newly formed company now produces more than half of the beer that is produced in Luxembourg.

SPECIFICATIONS
Brewery: Brasserie de Luxembourg Mousel-Diekirch
Location: Diekirch, Luxembourg
Style: Lager
Colour: Golden yellow
Alcohol: 4.8%
Serving temperature: 6°–8°C (42.8°–46.4°F)
Food: Grilled chicken or pork steaks

Premium Pils Mousel

Brewing reached its peak in Luxembourg in the 1860s when the Grand Duchy had around 35 breweries.

Despite being sandwiched between two of the world's major brewing nations, Germany and Belgium, it now has fewer than 10. Until it closed in 1999, Mousel (or Les Brasseries Réunies de Luxembourg Mousel et Clausen, to give it its full name) was one of the oldest, dating back to 1511, and the brewery originally stood on the site of the abbey at Altenmünster. Its beers, now brewed at Diekirch, are a straightforward light-flavoured Premium Pils and an unfiltered Zwickelbier.

SPECIFICATIONS
Brewery: Brasserie de Luxembourg Mousel-Diekirch
Location: Diekirch, Luxembourg
Style: Lager
Colour: Golden yellow
Alcohol: 4.8%
Serving temperature: 6°–8°C (42.8°–46.4°F)
Food: Shellfish platters, light seafood dishes

Simon Dinkel

This is a unique lager from the viewpoint of both aroma and flavour. It pours well and has a large frothy head and a buttery, slightly citric aroma.

The flavour is honey-sweet, but not overpoweringly so, and there is a spicy edge to it. The colour is unfiltered hazy yellow, bringing harvest fields to mind. The taste is superbly full-bodied, unlike many bland, weak lagers that dominate the market. The Brasserie Simon is an independent brewery that produces a small range of beers, some of which are seasonal for drinking at Christmas. It is an old concern, and was founded in 1824 by Joseph Simon, whose name graces the street in which it is situated.

SPECIFICATIONS
Brewery: Brasserie Simon
Location: Wilz
Style: Lager
Colour: Medium gold
Alcohol: 4.5%
Serving temperature: 42°–46°F (6°–8°C)
Food: Serve as an apéritif, or drink with spicy foods

'n halve gar(r)e

Belgian Beers

Belgium is home to more styles and varieties of beer than any other country in the world. Famously, it is where you will find the authentic Trappist beers brewed under strict conditions at one of the six monasteries – Achel, Chimay, Orval, Rochefort, Westmalle, Westvleteren – exclusively allowed to use the name Trappist on their labels.

Belgium is also home to perhaps the most remarkable beer style in the world, a beer that due to its very nature could not be imitated anywhere else. This is lambic beer, beer that ferments spontaneously by the action of airborne wild yeasts that exist only in the Payottenland region to Brussels' west. Lambic beers hark back thousands of years to the earliest days of brewing. The wort is left in open vessels overnight to be exposed to naturally occurring yeasts, then fermented in oak casks for up to two years, eventually creating a beer of incredible depth and complexity. Master brewers blend this with other lambics and sometimes fruit flavourings to make Gueuze.

In many respects Belgium's brewing industry is thriving, dynamic and healthy, but it is subject to the same global market forces that have seen the bulk of world brewing consolidated into the hands of a few major conglomerates. By far the largest stake in the Belgian brewing industry is held by Interbrew, which joined forces with AmBev in 2004. Scottish & Newcastle is the other major player. Still, new brewery openings continue to outnumber closures and, as long as people remain enthusiastic about the country's many wonderful, unique beers, there will always be a place for the smaller players.

Left: Belgium is one of the homes of world beer, producing varieties of ales, porters and lagers which are a connoisseur's delight. The bars in which the beers are served can often be as distinctive as the drinks, many of them being centuries old.

Above: Belgium's brewers are justifiably proud of the tremendous variety of beers that are produced within the country's borders and exported worldwide. Belgium is a prime destination for all beer lovers.

STATISTICS

Total production: 15,650,000 hectolitres (413,429,000 gallons) per year

Consumption per capita: 98 litres (26 gallons) per year

Famous breweries: Artois; Brasserie du Bocq; Brasserie de Rochefort; Brouwerij Duvel Moortgat NV; Brouwerij van Hoegaarden; Lindemans Farm Brewery; NV Brouwerijen Alken-Maes Brasseries SA

Famous brands: Abbaye des Rocs; Duvel Verde; Grimbergen Blonde; Hoegaarden; La Chouffe Blonde; Lindemans Framboise; Leffe Brune; Satan Gold; Stella Artois

Abbaye des Rocs

Set in a small picturesque village close to the French border, this small commercial brewery takes its name from the ruins of a nearby abbey.

It began brewing in 1979, producing a range of characterful strong ales in a variety of styles, the chief of which is the double-fermented ale of the same name, made using seven types of malt and aromatized with Belgian, German and Czech hop varieties. It is a rich, malty brew with complex yet subtle red wine characteristics, a sweet fruity aroma and a sharp palate with traces of burnt wood, dark fruit and bitter hops. The brewery also produces a strong unfiltered wheat beer, Blanche des Honelles, notable for its use of malted oats, as well as wheat and barley.

SPECIFICATIONS

Brewery: Brasserie de l'Abbaye des Rocs SA

Location: Montignies-sur-Roc, Hainaut

Style: Belgian abbey double

Colour: Dark red-brown

Alcohol: 9%

Serving temperature: 14°C (57.2°F)

Food: A rich, spicy fruit cake

La Chouffe Blonde

The Achouffe brewery began in 1982, as a hobby for two brothers-in-law, Pierre Gobron and Chris Bauweraerts.

Then in 1984 Pierre gave up his job to work full-time at the brewery. Chris joined him in 1988, and before long the brothers had a thriving business both domestically and in international exports. La Chouffe Blonde is an unpasteurized, bottle-conditioned strong golden ale, spiced with coriander and lightly hopped for a refreshing taste. The brewery also produces McChouffe, which is a strong, dark ale that may have a Scottish sounding name, but bears little resemblance to the 'Scotch' ales that are popular throughout Belgium, and Esprit d'Achouffe, which is an eau de vie that is distilled from five-year-old beer.

SPECIFICATIONS

Brewery: Brasserie d'Achouffe

Location: Achouffe, Luxembourg

Style: Golden ale

Colour: Amber-gold

Alcohol: 8%

Serving temperature: 12°C (53.6°F)

Food: Hot, spicy dishes

Leffe Brune

Leffe beers come in four distinct varieties. The most popular is Leffe Brune, a robust brown ale with a rich aroma of roasted caramel and hints of chocolate and dark fruit, and a slightly sweet finish that is reminiscent of raisins, balanced by spicy hop dryness.

The Leffe brand is the best known of all the Belgian 'abbey' beers. Unlike the authentic Trappist beers, these are not genuine monastic products, but the result of a commercial arrangement whereby a brewery produces the beers under licence, with the proceeds split between brewer and abbey. The Abbaye Notre Dame de Leffe was founded in 1152 in the town of Dinant, near Namur; brewing started on the site in the thirteenth century. Of the other three Leffe beers, the most significant is Leffe Blonde, a pale golden ale.

SPECIFICATIONS

Brewery: Abbaye de Leffe SA
Location: Leffe, Namur
Style: Belgian abbey brown ale
Colour: Brown
Alcohol: 6.5%
Serving temperature: 10°C (50°F)
Food: A hearty beef casserole

Stella Artois

Stella Artois, produced by the Artois brewery in Leuven, is one of the world's most recognizable lager brands. It is an all-malt pilsener-style bottom-fermented lager with a full-bodied, well-balanced character and a light, refreshing flavour belying its strength.

Stella Artois can trace its roots back to 1366, with the foundation of the Den Horen brewery in Leuven. In 1708, the title of Master Brewer of Den Horen passed to Sebastien Artois, and nine years later he bought the brewery outright. The original brewery was destroyed by artillery fire in World War I, but was rebuilt on the same site; in 1926 the company's most famous product was launched, named Stella from the Latin for 'star'.

SPECIFICATIONS

Brewery: Artois
Location: Leuven, Brabant
Style: Strong pilsener-style lager
Colour: Pale golden
Alcohol: 5.2%
Serving temperature: 6°C (43°F)
Food: Fried or grilled fish

Maes Pils

The Maes brewery was founded in 1880 when the ambitious Egid Maes took over the ailing Sint Michäel de Waarloos brewery.

It was principally an ale brewer until 1946, when it first introduced Maes Pils, a light, crisp lager with a mellow flavour. The history of Maes is a litany of brewery acquisitions and mergers. In 1988, Maes merged with Alken, the brewery that had introduced Cristal Alken in 1929, the first pilsener-style lager to be brewed in Belgium. The new company, Alken-Maes, remained in control of the Maes family until 1993, and since 2000 has been owned by Scottish & Newcastle.

SPECIFICATIONS
Brewery: Brouwerij Alken-Maes
Location: Alken, Limburg
Style: Pilsener-style lager
Colour: Pale yellow
Alcohol: 4.9%
Serving temperature: 6°–8°C (42.8°–46.4°F)
Food: Grilled fish and seafood

Petrus Winterbier

Petrus is the name given to the range of top-fermented ales from the Bavik brewery, including this seasonal version brewed during November. The aroma is soft and malty with a lightly roasted, slightly sweet character.

It has a subtle blend of spices, balanced with a citrussy hop dryness and a caramel malt sweetness. As well as the seasonal beer, Bavik brews four other ales under the Petrus label. The first was Oud Bruin, introduced in 1975, a deep, dark red beer made from a blend of brown ale and beer that has been aged in oak casks for a full two years. There is also a traditional amber-coloured ale called Speciale, and an elegant blond Tripel.

SPECIFICATIONS
Brewery: Brouwerij Bavik
Location: Bavikhove, West Flanders
Style: Strong dark ale
Colour: Copper red-brown
Alcohol: 6.5%
Serving temperature: 8°–10°C (46.4°–50°F)
Food: Hearty soups or barbecued meat

Satan Gold

The De Block brewing family has a long and illustrious history stretching back to the fourteenth century, when Henricus De Bloc was granted the right to brew beer for the Duke of Brabant and Burgundy. In 1887 one of his descendants, Louis De Block, founded the modern-day brewery in the small hamlet of Peizegem.

The brewery currently produces four regular beers, of which the two under the Satan label are its most popular. Satan Gold is a strong blond ale brewed with a blend of pale malts for a soft, fruity character balanced with a touch of spicy bitterness provided by subtle use of hops and spices. Satan Red uses dark malts and a similar blend of spices and fragrant hops, to produce a creamy dark ale.

SPECIFICATIONS

Brewery: Brouwerij De Block-Joostens
Location: Peizegem, Flemish Brabant
Style: Strong Belgian pale ale
Colour: Golden amber
Alcohol: 8%
Serving temperature: 8°–10°C (46.4°–50°F)
Food: Pizza or spicy Mexican food

Blanche de Namur

Blanche de Namur is a mild, refreshing, golden wheat beer that possesses a smooth fruity flavour with a hint of coriander spice and bitter orange.

It is part of the regular range of the du Bocq brewery, the origins of which date back to 1858, when farmer Martin Belot started brewing his own beer on his farm in the village of Purnode, close to Dinant. Originally a project to keep his workers occupied during the winter months, the brewing side of the business soon took over and the farm was closed down in 1960. The Du Bocq brewery remains an independent family-run concern to this day.

SPECIFICATIONS

Brewery: Brasserie du Bocq
Location: Purnode, Namur
Style: Belgian witbier / wheat beer
Colour: Hazy golden yellow
Alcohol: 4.5%
Serving temperature: 6°C (42.8°F)
Food: Fish, white meat and poultry

Pauwel Kwak

Every Belgian brewery traditionally markets its own distinctive shape of glass, which is supposed to be the ideal vessel for drinking its particular beers.

None, however, is as distinctive as the hourglass-shaped round-bottomed flagon in which Pauwel Kwak is served. It is modelled on the stirrup cup served to coach drivers on horseback, who could take a sip, then set the glass in their stirrup, and was inspired by a legendary innkeeper who was famous for a strong ale similar to the one that now bears his name. Brewed with three types of malt and sweetened with candy sugar, it is rich and warming with a caramel malt character.

SPECIFICATIONS
Brewery: Brouwerij Bosteels
Location: Buggenhout, East Flanders
Style: Strong Belgian ale
Colour: Golden amber-red
Alcohol: 8%
Serving temperature: 13°C (55.4°F)
Food: Dark chocolate

Chimay Bleue

Originally brewed as a Christmas beer, Chimay Bleue is both the strongest and the most popular of the three beers produced at the most famous of Belgium's trappist breweries.

A classic strong, dark, warming winter ale, top-fermented with secondary fermentation in the bottle, it keeps well in the bottle for at least five years, maturing to become smoother and drier in the style of a good port. Hints of caramel and a fresh, light floral and yeasty aroma give way to rich fruit, spice and roasted malt flavours on the palate. The name comes from the distinctive blue cap on the bottle (the other Chimay beers have red and white caps), but Chimay Bleue is also available in larger corked bottles, labelled as Chimay Grande Reserve.

SPECIFICATIONS
Brewery: Bières de Chimay SA
Location: Abbaye de Notre Dame de Scourmont, Chimay, Hainaut
Style: Strong dark Belgian abbey ale (Trappist)
Colour: Deep copper
Alcohol: 9%
Serving temperature: 14°C (57.2°F)
Food: An after-dinner beer to enjoy with a cigar

Moinette Blonde

The Moinette name, from the French for 'monk', is applied to the Dupont brewery's range of strong ales. As is typical of many Belgian breweries, Dupont's ales come in Blonde and Brune (brown) versions, both of which weigh in at 8.5% alcohol.

The Blonde version has a spicy hop aroma balanced with a sweet malty flavour; the Brune has more of a roasted malt character with a hint of burnt caramel and natural spiciness in the flavour. Dedicated to traditional methods of beer production, Dupont matures all of its beers in warm cellars for two months and bottles them unfiltered and unpasteurized, giving them a characteristic cloudiness. Since 1990, the brewery has also been leading the way in organic brewing.

SPECIFICATIONS

Brewery: Brasserie Dupont sprl
Location: Tourpes-Leuze, Hainaut
Style: Strong ale
Colour: Pale golden yellow
Alcohol: 8.5%
Serving temperature: 10°–12°C (50°–53.6°F)
Food: Barbecued meats

Hoegaarden Blanche

Belgium's main wheat-growing region once boasted more than 30 breweries that all made a distinctive spiced wheat beer – a style which had died out completely by the late 1950s.

Fortunately, they were not gone for long. Pierre Celis grew up in the town of Hoegaarden next door to the Tomsin brewery, the last of the wheat beer breweries to close. Determined to revive his favourite beer style, he started brewing Hoegaarden in 1966; the current popularity of wheat beers around the world is entirely to his credit. Flavoured with coriander seed and Curaçao orange peel, the beer is light and refreshing.

SPECIFICATIONS

Brewery: Brouwerij van Hoegaarden
Location: Hoegaarden
Style: Belgian wheat beer
Colour: Cloudy golden orange-yellow
Alcohol: 5%
Serving temperature: 9°–10°C (48.2°–50°F)
Food: Grilled chicken with light vegetable accompaniment

Lindemans Framboise

Southwest of Brussels, in the quiet Belgian town of Vlezenbeek, the Lindemans family has been farming and home brewing as long as anyone can remember. Commercial brewing started in 1811.

Lambic, or spontaneously fermented beers, are among the world's rarest. These products mature in oak for nearly two years prior to release. Long before hops were common, various fruits and vegetables were used to season beers. Lambic beer's acidity blends perfectly with raspberries. Framboise has a magnificent aroma, a delicate palate of raspberries with undertones of fruity acidity, and an elegant, sparkling clean natural taste.

SPECIFICATIONS

Brewery: Lindemans Farm Brewery
Location: Vlezenbeek, Flemish Brabant
Style: Raspberry lambic
Colour: Rose
Alcohol: 3.8%
Serving temperature: 7.2°C (45°F)
Food: Chocolate desserts, fresh raspberries, ice cream with a raspberry demi-glaze sauce, Crème Caramel, Baked Alaska, oysters, caviar

Duvel

Duvel is famous for its potent hop aroma and despite its high alcohol content is a surprisingly refreshing, easy-drinking beer, stone dry with fragrant, zesty fruit aromas and flavour.

In 1918, Albert Moortgat decided to brew a beer similar to the pale ales brought over by the British troops during World War I. After much experimentation, the beer was launched in 1923 as Victory Ale, but upon tasting the new beer one brewery worker proclaimed, 'Da's nen echten duvel' ('That's a devil of a beer'), and so it thereafter came to be known as Duvel.

SPECIFICATIONS

Brewery: Brouwerij Duvel Moortgat NV
Location: Breendonk-Puurs, Antwerp
Style: Belgian strong blonde ale
Colour: Pale golden straw yellow
Alcohol: 8.5%
Serving temperature: 10°C (50°F)
Food: Serve on its own as a pre-dinner apéritif

Duvel Verde

The original unfiltered, bottle-conditioned Duvel comes in large (three-litre) or small (33cl) bottles with a red cap and red lettering on the label and is sometimes known as Duvel Rood.

Duvel Verde is a pasteurized, filtered version of the same beer, available only in the smaller size and brewed to a slightly lower alcoholic strength. Moortgat also produces a crisp, dry Belgian-style pilsener called Vedette, as well as a stronger Bavarian-style pilsener with a more pronounced hop character known as Bel Pils and an amber-blond ale called Passendale, launched in 2000 as a joint venture with the manufacturers of a cheese by the same name.

SPECIFICATIONS

Brewery: Brouwerij Duvel Moortgat NV
Location: Breendonk-Puurs, Antwerp
Style: Belgian strong golden ale
Colour: Pale golden yellow
Alcohol: 8%
Serving temperature: 10°C (50°F)
Food: A crisp, green salad

Lucifer

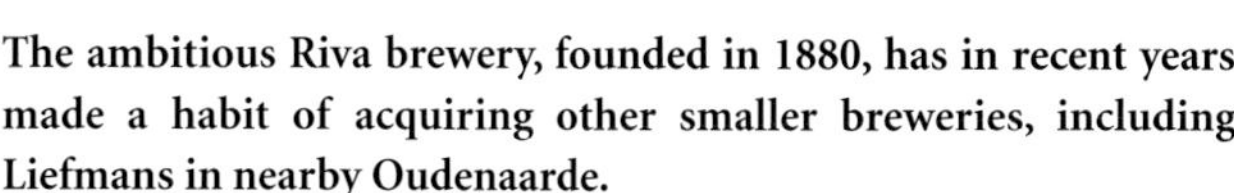

The ambitious Riva brewery, founded in 1880, has in recent years made a habit of acquiring other smaller breweries, including Liefmans in nearby Oudenaarde.

From its own range, its Dentergem Witbier is one of the biggest selling examples of a cloudy spiced wheat beer, and has a smooth, dry flavour. Lucifer is a strong, golden ale that imitates its rival Duvel in more than just its diabolical name. The aroma is spicy and fruity with hints of cloves, citrus fruit and apple, while the smooth, medium-bodied palate is well balanced between zesty hops and sweet, toasty malts.

SPECIFICATIONS

Brewery: Brouwerij Riva SA
Location: Dentergem, West Flanders province
Style: Belgian strong blonde ale
Colour: Golden yellow-orange
Alcohol: 8%
Serving temperature: 10°C (50°F)
Food: Hot, spicy food, Chinese curries

Grimbergen Blonde

Produced by Alken-Maes, this is a strong blond beer, with a yeasty softness to the palate that is reminiscent of Trappist beers, and a tenacious, frothy head.

It has a slightly hoppy aroma, which is less pronounced in the taste. Quite sweet, but not overpoweringly so, with a strong hint of vanilla in the aftertaste, Grimbergen Blonde is very drinkable, but not in quantity due to the strength. This is a complex and enjoyable Belgian ale, and well worth rooting out. According to tradition, Grimbergen Blonde is based on an ancient recipe brewed at Grimbergen Abbey in 1128. The Alken-Maes Brewery, meanwhile, dates back to 1880 and was established from two local breweries.

SPECIFICATIONS

Brewery: NV Brouwerijen Alken-Maes Brasseries SA
Location: Jumet, Hainaut
Style: Strong ale
Colour: Light blonde
Alcohol: 6.7%
Serving temperature: 7.2°C(45°F)
Food: Roast lamb, beef stews

Timmermans Kriek

Although the term 'Kriek' has come to mean any beer which is flavoured with cherries, the version from Timmermans is an authentic lambic beer, produced by the action of naturally occurring yeasts, in which whole cherries have been steeped during maturation.

A relatively easy-drinking example of the style, it has a pleasantly sweet cherry flavour balanced with a dry sherry-like acidity characteristic of true lambic beers. Various other flavoured lambics are also available, including a dry, full-flavoured Framboise (raspberry), a Cassis (blackcurrant) and a Pêche (peach). The brewery also produces an innovative 'white' lambic, which is a blend of lambic and wheat beers.

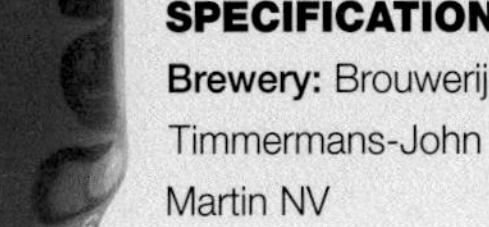

SPECIFICATIONS

Brewery: Brouwerij Timmermans-John Martin NV
Location: Itterbeek
Style: Kriek (cherry) lambic
Colour: Bright cherry red
Alcohol: 5%
Serving temperature: 8°–9°C (46.4°–48.2°F)
Food: Light fruity desserts such as soufflés

Trappistes Rochefort 8

Of the six Trappist monasteries that brew commercially, the Abbaye de Notre Dame de Saint-Remy on the outskirts of Rochefort is the most traditional and secretive, and little is known to the outside world of the monks who produce the beer.

What is well documented is that a convent was founded on the site in 1230 and converted to a monastery in 1464, with brewing taking place here since the late sixteenth century. Brasserie de Rochefort beers are also among the most individual, being rich, dark and malty, and flavoured with a highly secret blend of spices. Candy sugar is added to the beer before bottling to promote secondary fermentation, and each batch of beer is given up to 10 weeks of maturation.

SPECIFICATIONS

Brewery: Brasserie de Rochefort
Location: Abbaye de Notre Dame de Saint-Rémy, Rochefort, Namur
Style: Belgian abbey tripel (Trappist)
Colour: Copper-brown
Alcohol: 9.2%
Serving temperature: 10°–14°C (50°–57.2°F)
Food: A good all-round beer, goes well with sausages

Westmalle Trappist Dubbel

Brewed at the Trappist abbey of Westmalle, north of Antwerp, Westmalle Trappist Dubbel pours to a somewhat hazy, rich, dark, peaty colour with traces of amber and a large and foamy, pale tan head which lasts well and leaves masses of lace on the glass.

Initial aromas are sweet malt and a yeasty, bready tone. There is a strong hop presence, but the overwhelming malt wins through with a fruity, ripe banana quality from the yeast backing it up. Westmalle is the largest of Belgium's six Trappist breweries and competes with Chimay for the title of most commercially oriented (although all profits go to good causes). It exports to 14 countries worldwide.

SPECIFICATIONS

Brewery: Brouwerij der Trappisten van Westmalle
Location: Westmalle
Style: Trappist beer
Colour: Rich amber
Alcohol: 6.5%
Serving temperature: 6.0°C (43°F)
Food: Rabbit, hare, small game

1719
BAVARIA

Dutch Beers

With Germany to the east and Belgium to the south, one might think that the brewing industry of the Netherlands would have benefited from the positive influence of its neighbours. Unfortunately, this has not always been so. One could argue that, while Belgian brewers concentrate on quality, their Dutch counterparts prefer quantity.

The prime exemplar of this is Heineken, formerly a small family brewer, but now a giant multinational corporation and the second-largest brewing company in the world, with a presence in one form or another in just about every beer-producing country in the world. The success of the company is largely down to one man: Alfred 'Freddie' Heineken, the grandson of the brewery's founder, who brought in a visionary approach to marketing and a strong business sense when he took charge of the company in the 1950s.

There are other breweries in the Netherlands apart from Heineken, but surprisingly few for a country with such a strong tradition for beer drinking. The situation today is not as bad as it was in the 1970s, when there were just two major players – Heineken and Skol – plus a handful of small regional brewers, all producing fairly unexciting blond lagers. More recently, Dutch beer consumers have developed a taste for more interesting beers. The popularity of imports from Belgium has inspired domestic brewers to start producing a wider variety of ales, lagers and even wheat beers, including several traditional seasonal specialities that had all but died out.

Left: Like Belgium, the Netherlands plays host to a rich tradition of beer brewing that also connects with the age-old Trappist techniques. The Bavaria pilsener pictured here is one of the more popular high-street bar and bottled varieties; but a large number of microbreweries produce more complex, darker ales.

Above: Pictured here is the De Hooiberg (the 'Haystack') brewery in Amsterdam (now a museum), where it all began for Heineken in 1863, when Gerard Adriaan Heineken bought the brewery and started the business which is now a giant in the world of brewing.

STATISTICS

Total production: 25,124,000 hectolitres(663,706,000 gallons) per year

Consumption per capita: 81 litres (21 gallons) per year

Famous breweries: Bavaria Brouwerij NV; Bierbrouwerij de Koningshoeven; Bierbrouwerij Sint Christoffel; Grolsch Bierbrouwerij NV; Heineken Brouwerij BV; Lindeboom Bierbrouwerij NV; Oranjeboom Bierbrouwerij

Famous brands: Bavaria; Christoffel Blond; Grolsch; Gulpener Dort; Heinenken; Lindeboom; Oranjeboom

Bavaria Premium Pilsener

Despite the name, the Netherlands' largest independent brewery has no Bavarian connections, although it claims to brew its pilsener according to Germany's strict purity laws.

It has a fresh, honeyed lemon aroma and a crisp, refreshing, slightly sweet grassy flavour balanced with a sharp hop bitterness leading to a dry finish. It is brewed with water from the brewery's own well and malted barley from its own maltings, and is the flagship beer of a brewery that can trace its origins back to 1719, when it was established by one Laurentius Moorees. The Swinkel family who have owned the brewery since the late nineteenth century are direct descendants of Laurentius. In recent years, Bavaria has expanded by buying up many smaller breweries, such as the famous Kroon brewery in Oirschot.

SPECIFICATIONS
Brewery: Bavaria Brouwerij NV
Location: Lieshout, North Brabant
Style: Pilsener
Colour: Golden yellow
Alcohol: 5%
Serving temperature: 6°–8°C (42.8°–46.4°F)
Food: Roast duck

Bavaria 8.6

Taking its name from its alcohol content, Bavaria 8.6 is the strongest beer in its range and also its most flavoursome.

Although it is a top-fermented lager, it shares many characteristics with a barley wine ale. It has a grainy, biscuity aroma with hints of vanilla and honey, and a sweet malty flavour balanced in the finish by a light hop bitterness, although it risks being overpowered by its high alcohol content. Bavaria mostly concentrates on bottom-fermented lagers, but does produce a full-flavoured top-fermented bock called Hooghe Bock, with a mild bittersweet flavour. The range also includes Oud Bruin, an old-fashioned brown beer with a caramel malt flavour that is similar to the beers from the brewery's early days.

SPECIFICATIONS
Brewery: Bavaria Brouwerij NV
Location: Lieshout, North Brabant
Style: Strong lager
Colour: Golden amber-yellow
Alcohol: 8.6%
Serving temperature: 10°–12°C (50°–53.6°F)
Food: Shortcrust pies

Amstel

Amstel pours a clear copper colour with a small foamy slightly off-white head. It exudes an aromatic floral nose hinting at violet blossoms with a touch of malts. The aroma becomes more noticeable as the beer becomes warmer.

The flavour is dry and slightly bitter; the body medium. The beer has a satisfying malty taste with a slight fruity background and a dry and hop-bitter finish of medium length. One of the attractions of Amstel is that it is a good deal darker than the more usual Pilsner, hinting that it holds something special in store. It certainly has more flavour than other comparable brews. Amstel is available both in bottled form and on tap.

SPECIFICATIONS
Brewery: Heineken Brouwerij BV
Location: Hertogenbosch
Style: Pilsener
Colour: Copper
Alcohol: 5.0%
Serving temperature: 6°–8°C (43°–46°F)
Food: Snacks, or drink as an apéritif

Gulpener Dort

The town of Gulpen, in the far southeastern tip of the Netherlands, is home to the independent family-run Gulpener Bierbrouwerij. In the hands of the Rutten family since it was founded in 1825, it is currently being run by the fifth generation of Ruttens.

A large stake in the company was purchased by Grolsch in 1995. This means that Gulpener beers now enjoy fairly widespread distribution, both domestically and in the export market. Gulpener continues to maintain its long-standing reputation for experimentation with a wide and varied range of beer styles. Gulpener Dort, for example, is brewed in the style of the strong export lagers of Dortmund, with a fuller body than a pilsener and a sweeter flavour. It has an aroma of dark fruit with plum and raisin notes and a similarly fruity flavour balanced by a fragrant hop bitterness.

SPECIFICATIONS
Brewery: Gulpener Bierbrouwerij
Location: Gulpen, Limburg
Style: Dortmunder / export lager
Colour: Clear orange-brown
Alcohol: 6.5%
Serving temperature: 8°–10°C (46.4°–50°F)
Food: Chargrilled chicken or lamb steaks

Heineken

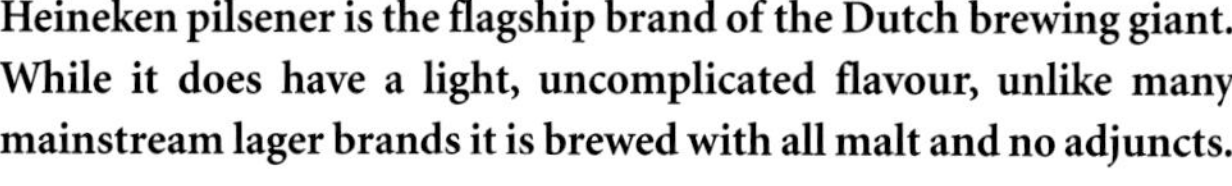

Heineken pilsener is the flagship brand of the Dutch brewing giant. While it does have a light, uncomplicated flavour, unlike many mainstream lager brands it is brewed with all malt and no adjuncts.

Heineken is not only the largest brewer in the Netherlands, but also the second-largest brewer in the world. The company was founded in 1864 by Gerard Adriaan Heineken; by 1942 Heineken was a public company and the family had lost its controlling stake. Alfred Henry Heineken, Gerard's grandson, was determined to buy back the family name and started by working in the brewery itself, carrying sacks of barley. He worked his way up and gradually bought up enough shares to regain a controlling interest in 1954. His story is key to Heineken's present-day success, much of which is due buying up smaller breweries, including famous old brands such as Amstel, Affligem and Brand.

SPECIFICATIONS
Brewery: Heineken Brouwerij BV
Location: Hertogenbosch
Style: Pilsener
Colour: Pale golden yellow
Alcohol: 5%
Serving temperature: 6°–8°C (42.8°–46.4°F)
Food: Minted lamb burgers

Grolsch

The flagship beer from the Grolsch brewery of Enschede, the largest independent brewer in the Netherlands, is a full-flavoured golden pilsener with a more bitter taste than most mainstream lagers.

The brewery claims its origins lie in the beer created by Peter Cuyper in 1615 to win the hand of the daughter of a local brewer, and it maintains its traditional image today with its distinctive embossed bottles with their flip-top lids. As well as its pilsener, Grolsch also brews various other beers for the domestic market, such as Het Canon, a rich amber-coloured malty barley wine.

SPECIFICATIONS
Brewery: Grolsch Bierbrouwerij NV
Location: Enschede, Overijssel
Style: Pilsener
Colour: Deep golden yellow
Alcohol: 5%
Serving temperature: 6°–8°C (42.8°–46.4°F)
Food: Serve as an apéritif

La Trappe Blond

When the Trappist monks were expelled from France during the Revolution, most of them moved north to the Lowlands, settling in Belgium. One group moved further north, building a new abbey near Tilburg.

The brewery, originally called Schaapskooi (meaning 'sheep fold'), was formed in 1881, but today its status as an authentic Trappist brewery is in dispute – it is currently owned and operated by Bavaria, who label the beers Trappist despite limited involvement from the monks. In any case, its beers are highly regarded. La Trappe Blond is a top-fermented golden ale with an aromatic bitter hop aroma, which also conveys citrussy overtones, and a refreshing bitter flavour balanced by fruity malts.

SPECIFICATIONS

Brewery: Bierbrouwerij de Koningshoeven
Location: Berkel-Enschot, North Brabant
Style: Abbey blond ale
Colour: Cloudy pale straw yellow
Alcohol: 6.5%
Serving temperature: 8°–10°C (46.4°–50°F)
Food: Meatballs

La Trappe Quadrupel

La Trappe Quadrupel is one of the most powerful of the La Trappe beers, weighing in at 10% abv.

'Quadrupel' is a label given to very strong abbey or Trappist ale, the other type of strong abbey ale being the Abt. The difference between the Abt and the Quadrupel is that the former has a darker colour and deeper, more complex aromas and palate, while the latter has a lighter colour and texture, with more flavours of peach emerging. Both Abt and Quadrupel share the same power, 10% abv being the typical alcohol content, and the beers are generally bottle-conditioned. La Trappe Quadrupel is a seasonal beer, available in autumn and winter.

SPECIFICATIONS

Brewery: Bierbrouwerij de Koningshoeven
Location: Berkel-Enschot, North Brabant
Style: Abbey quadrupel
Colour: Rich amber
Alcohol: 10%
Serving temperature: 10°–12°C (50°–53.6°F)
Food: Spicy sausages

Lindeboom Pilsener

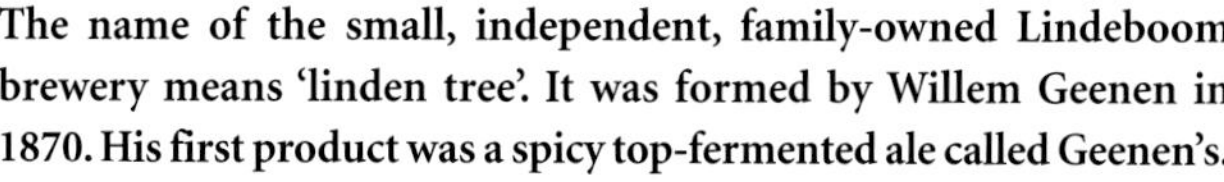

The name of the small, independent, family-owned Lindeboom brewery means 'linden tree'. It was formed by Willem Geenen in 1870. His first product was a spicy top-fermented ale called Geenen's.

In 1912 Geenen's sons, Bernard and Christien, now in charge of the company, christened the opening of their new brewing plant with the launch of Lindeboom Pilsener. Made with a blend of two types of pale malt and aromatized with a generous helping of whole German hops, it is a well-flavoured beer with more bitterness than most mainstream pilseners. Lindeboom's full range extends to Oud Bruin, a sweet flavoured malty brown ale, and Venloosch Alt, an authentic red-brown ale in the style of Düsseldorf's top-fermented, cold-conditioned altbiers. The brewery is now managed by another Willem Geenen, grandson of the founder.

SPECIFICATIONS	
Brewery: Lindeboom Bierbrouwerij NV	**Colour:** Pale golden yellow
Location: Neer, Limburg	**Alcohol:** 5%
Style: Pilsener	**Serving temperature:** 6°–8°C (42.8°–46.4°F)
	Food: Bacon quiche

Oranjeboom Premium Pilsener

This is a steady middle-of-the-road light lager that pours well, but produces a head that seems to vary from weak to long-lasting, depending where the beer is stored and under what conditions. The aroma is quite good and zesty; hops are prominent but not overpowering, and there is an underlying sweetness.

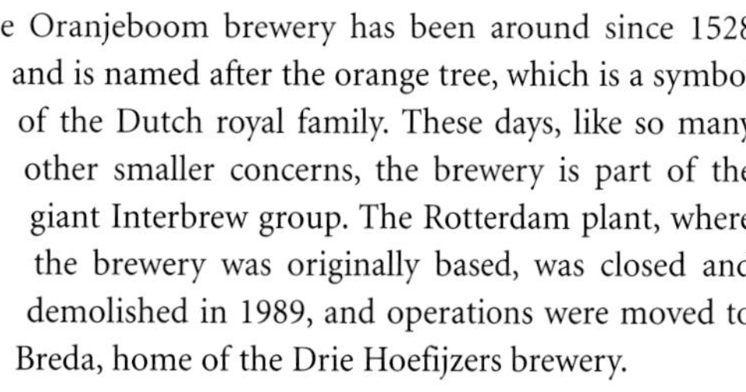

The Oranjeboom brewery has been around since 1528 and is named after the orange tree, which is a symbol of the Dutch royal family. These days, like so many other smaller concerns, the brewery is part of the giant Interbrew group. The Rotterdam plant, where the brewery was originally based, was closed and demolished in 1989, and operations were moved to Breda, home of the Drie Hoefijzers brewery.

SPECIFICATIONS	
Brewery: Brouwerij Oranjeboom (InBev)	**Colour:** Gold
Location: Breda	**Alcohol:** 5.0%
Style: Pilsener	**Serving temperature:** 6°–8°C (43°–46°F)
	Food: Serve as an apéritif

Oranjeboom Oud Bruin

Sweetened and coloured with caramel, the Netherland's traditional Oud Bruin beers are always relatively low in alcohol, and are particularly popular with elderly residents of the Limburg region.

Oranjeboom Oud Bruin is a bottom-fermented beer that pours with a small, frothy tan head. It has a metallic nose and a very sugary flavour, typical of most low-alcohol beers. In terms of alcoholic content, Oranjeboom Oud Bruin is only 2.5%, around half the strength of a typical high-street lager. As such it can be a good accompaniment to the lightest of snacks and meals, such as pancakes, when alcohol intake needs to be kept to a minimum.

SPECIFICATIONS
Brewery: Brouwerij Oranjeboom (InBev)
Location: Breda
Style: Dark lager
Colour: Brown
Alcohol: 2.5%
Serving temperature: 6°–8°C (43°–46°F)
Food: Pancakes

Christoffel Blond

The first beer to come from the Sint Christoffel brewery was simply called Christoffel Bier, but was renamed to Christoffel Blond when the brewery introduced Robertus to the range.

Blond is a full-bodied, pale golden pilsener-style lager with a well-balanced flavour characterized by a robust, fragrant hop bitterness. Unfiltered and unpasteurized, it develops further as it matures in the bottle. Sint Christoffel was founded in the former coalmining town of Roermond in 1986 by Leo Brand, a member of the famous Brand brewing family. Starting as a tiny operation, it quickly grew and is now one of the most successful of a new wave of Dutch breweries adhering to traditional values for quality beer production.

SPECIFICATIONS
Brewery: Bierbrouwerij Sint Christoffel

Location: Roermond, Limburg
Style: Pilsener
Colour: Pale golden yellow
Alcohol: 6%
Serving temperature: 8°C (46.4°F)
Food: Lasagne

BERTOZZI
JUWELIER
Augustiner
laura ashley
Wernle

Swiss Beers

Swiss beer production still has a local feel, with individual areas being served by regional breweries and even by microbreweries. Generally speaking, light lager-style beers predominate in Switzerland, but this appeal to popularity did not stop a slight decline (0.4%) in beer consumption across the nation between 1998 and 2003.

In general, Swiss beer bears a close resemblance to that produced in neighbouring Austria and Bavaria. There are two distinct beer-producing regions in the country: the cantons (counties) of the west, where the language is predominantly French, and the German-speaking cantons of eastern Switzerland. In the west, the industry is heavily influenced by imports from Belgium and other French-speaking parts of the world, including Quebec, but rather surprisingly there is also a distinct British influence, with various British styles being produced in microbreweries. Eastern Switzerland, on the other hand, in keeping with its strong German tradition, is very much lager country. In fact many of the breweries observe Germany's strict Reinheitsgebot purity laws. Swiss law allows the use of maize and rice, as well as up to 10% sugar and 20% starch.

Brewing in Switzerland is diversified through the proliferation of microbreweries attached to public houses. Increasingly professional in both product and marketing, using websites to make local and even international sales of their beers, these microbreweries have become potential big players of the future, as well as keeping alive the best traditions of Swiss beer producing. In 2003 the three biggest beer producers in Switzerland were Feldschlosschen, Heineken and Eichoff. Not surprisingly, large international brewing companies have made inroads into Switzerland, and now more than two-thirds of the Swiss beer market is held by Carlsberg and Heineken.

Left: A typical street scene in Switzerland's largest city, Zurich. The most popular type of beer in eastern Switzerland is a pale, easy-drinking lager generally referred to by the German term of 'Helles', meaning in this context 'light in colour' and which other European countries might usually call a 'Pils', a term that is rarely used in Switzerland.

Above: A typical Swiss bar is seen here. These usually serve a mix of popular branded lager beers, but they do sometimes sell brews from in-house microbreweries.

STATISTICS

Total production: 3,645,000 hectolitres (96,291,000 gallons) per year
Consumption per capita: 57 litres (15 gallons) per year
Famous breweries: Brauerei Eichhof; Brauerei Feldschlösschen
Famous brands: Eichhof Hubertus; Original Draft Cardinal; Original Feldschlösschen

Altes Tramdepot Tram-Märzen

As its name suggests, Altes Tramdepot is a brewpub situated in an old tram garage. In addition to the three regular draught beers (Tram-Helles, Tram-Märzen and Tram-Weizen, all of which are also available in bottled form), it produces seasonal specialities such as English Bitter Ale, Pils, Oktoberfestbier, Trappist Beer, Smoked Beer, Münchner and Easter Bock.

At 4.7% alcohol Tram-Märzen is stronger than most Oktoberfest brews. It produces a light hop and malt aroma, with a hint of spices, and there is an orange aftertaste. This is a well-structured beer, with well-defined flavours. The Altes Tramdepot Brewery and Brasserie was established in 1999 and offers excellent cuisine and wonderful views of the city.

SPECIFICATIONS
Brewery: Altes Tramdepot
Location: Berne
Style: Oktoberfest Märzen
Colour: Amber
Alcohol: 4.7%
Serving temperature: 10°C (50°F)
Food: Sausages, sliced veal, pastries

Original Draft Cardinal

One of the first commercial breweries in Switzerland, Cardinal was founded in Freiburg in 1788, when local landlord François Piller built a brewery next to his tavern.

In 1890, Freiburg's bishop was ordained as a cardinal, and the brewery produced a special beer to commemorate the event, later renaming the brewery in its honour. By 1996, the Feldschlösschen brewing group had taken over Cardinal and threatened to close the historic brewery until local pressure stopped this. Original Draft Cardinal is a well-balanced, lightly hopped lager with a soft, mellow flavour. The brewery also produces a fuller flavoured Spéciale and seasonal beers.

SPECIFICATIONS
Brewery: Brasserie du Cardinal
Location: Fribourg
Style: Lager
Colour: Pale yellow
Alcohol: 4.9%
Serving temperature: 6°–8°C (42.8°–46.4°F)
Food: Crisp, green salad

Eichhof Hubertus

Hubertus is a strong dark lager from Lucerne's Eichhof brewery, one of Switzerland's growing beer production companies. Its golden brown colour, which also has reddish tints, comes from the fact that it is made with roasted malts, which are also apparent in the full, rich roasted malt aroma.

For a popular lager Hubertus has a good deal of alcoholic power, but its alcohol content does not mask the flavours and aromas. Eichhof produces a wide range of beers of varying styles and strengths. Braugold is a bright golden lager with a herbal hop aroma and flavour; another popular beer is the pilsener-style Pony, which has an even more pronounced hop character and a complex flavour characterized by a refreshing bitterness. Other brands include Braugold (pale lager), Spiess Edelhell (pale lager) and Barbara (premium lager).

SPECIFICATIONS
Brewery: Brauerei Eichhof
Location: Lucerne
Style: Dark lager
Colour: Golden brown
Alcohol: 5.7%
Serving temperature: 8°–10°C (46.4°–50°F)
Food: Cold cooked meats

Original Feldschlösschen

Original Feldschlösschen is a classic bottom-fermented lager, well balanced and thirst-quenching, with a refreshing malty flavour and a slight touch of hop bitterness.

Feldschlösschen was founded in 1877 in Rheinfelden, near Basel, by two local men, Mathias Wütrich and Theophil Roniger, and remained in the ownership of Wütrich's descendants until the 1990s. By 1898, Feldschlösschen had become Switzerland's largest brewer. It enhanced that status by merging with its main rivals, Cardinal in 1992 and Hürlimann in 1996. The Feldschlösschen group has also absorbed several smaller brands, including Warteck and Gurten.

SPECIFICATIONS
Brewery: Brauerei Feldschlösschen
Location: Rheinfelden
Style: Lager
Colour: Pale yellow
Alcohol: 4.8%
Serving temperature: 6°–8°C (42.8°–46.4°F)
Food: Sausages and pretzels

HB
MÜNCHEN

German Beers

No country takes more pride in the quality of its beers than Germany, a pride that is embodied in the Reinheitsgebot purity laws. First introduced in Bavaria in 1516 by Duke William IV, the law stipulated that beer could be made with only three ingredients: water, barley and hops.

The ruling had to be amended later when the discovery was made of the importance of yeast in brewing, and was further amended to permit the use of wheat. The Reinheitsgebot has in recent years come under fire, in particular from the French who in 1987 forced the European Parliament to rule that it was a barrier to trade. Despite this, many German brewers continue to abide by the principle, enabling them to distinguish their beers from mass-market cheap lagers, even if it does mean that German beers tend to show a conservative character, lacking the innovation of modern beers brewed in Belgium, the United Kingdom and the United States.

This conservatism is further reinforced by the German habit of preferring the local beer style, which has led to different beers being closely associated with their city of origin – the strong, malty export beers of Dortmund, the altbiers of Düsseldorf, the top-fermented Kölsch ales of Cologne and the dark lager of Munich. Despite this, Germany can proudly boast some of the world's most distinctive beers, among them Rauchbier (smoke beer), a speciality of the town of Bamberg in the Franconia region, and the Schwarzbier (black beer) of eastern Germany. It is also famous for the Munich Oktoberfest, which takes place for 16 days every year. Only Munich's six main breweries are allowed to sell their beers at the Oktoberfest; one of these, Spaten, created a special beer for the festival in 1882, which has since become a classic.

Left: The cold, icy caves at the foothills of the Alps gave German brewers the perfect spot for storing beer. When they brewed their last beer in March, they brewed enough for all the months until October. They stored the excess in the caves and celebrated with a party at the end of the summer.

Above: German beer has an almost unrivalled range of brands and speciality brews, some of which have centuries of history behind them.

STATISTICS

Total production: 106,304,000 hectolitres (2,808,255,000 gallons) per year
Consumption per capita: 122 litres (32 gallons) per year
Famous breweries: Brauerei Beck; Brauerei Weihenstephan; Löwenbräu AG; Paulaner GmbH;
Famous brands: Beck's; Bitburger Premium; DAB Original; Edeldstoff Augustiner; Erdinger Wiessbier; Jever Pilsener; Löwenbräu; Spaten Munchen; Wernesgrüner

Andechser Bergbock Hell

Beer has been brewed at the small town of Andechs in Upper Bavaria's Five Lakes region since 1455, when the Benedictine monastery was founded by Duke Albrecht III on Andechs mountain, overlooking Lake Ammersee.

Beer production took place at the monastery itself until 1972, when a dedicated modern brewery was built at the foot of the mountain. It has since gone from strength to strength, supporting not only the monastery but also the whole of the local economy. The brewery's beers can be sampled on tap in the Bräustüberl (brewery pub) or Klostergasthof (monastery restaurant). Bergbock Hell displays all the typical characteristics of a light-coloured bock (strong) beer. Other Andechs beers include a 'Spezial' Hell in the classic Oktoberfest style.

SPECIFICATIONS
Brewery: Andechs Klosterbrauerei
Location: Andechs, Bavaria
Style: Bock
Colour: Deep yellow
Alcohol: 6.9%
Serving temperature: 9°–10° C (48.2°–50°F)
Food: The meatloaf produced by the monastery's butchery

Edelstoff Augustiner

This crisp lager comes from the historic Augustiner brewery of Munich. The city's Augustinian monastery was founded in 1294 and records show that its brewery was in existence by 1328.

In 1803 the monastery was dissolved, along with many others, by Napoleon, although brewing and selling of beer in the monastery tavern continued, with the brewery moving to its present site in 1817. Augustiner is one of six breweries allowed to brew a beer for the famous Oktoberfest celebrations that take place in Munich every year. As well as the Edelstoff and the Oktoberfest beers, Augustiner produces, among others, a rich, warming abbey-style double bock called Maximator, available in winter.

SPECIFICATIONS
Brewery: Augustiner Bräu
Location: Munich, Bavaria
Style: Dortmunder/export
Colour: Pale amber-gold
Alcohol: 5.6%
Serving temperature: 8°–9°C (46.4°–48.2°F)
Food: Grilled or fried chicken or rabbit

Ayinger Bräu-Weisse

This unfiltered wheat beer is a first-class example of the style, characteristically cloudy with yeast sediment and pouring with a deep, billowing head. It has a potent aroma of bananas and lemon with underlying hints of cloves, and a refreshingly crisp, tart flavour reminiscent of green apples.

The Aying brewery also produces a rich, malty dark lager in the classic Bavarian style, and a popular doppelbock called Celebrator, as well as several other styles. The brewery was established in 1877. Although it started off small, production soon increased and, when the rail link to nearby Munich was built it brought tourists to Aying, many of whom stayed at the Brauereigasthof (brewery guesthouse).

SPECIFICATIONS
Brewery: Aying Brauerei
Location: Aying, Bavaria
Style: Hefe-Weizen / Weissbier
Colour: Cloudy, pale straw colour
Alcohol: 5.1%
Serving temperature: 8°–10° C (46.4°–50°F)
Food: The regional speciality, weisswurst sausage

Beck's

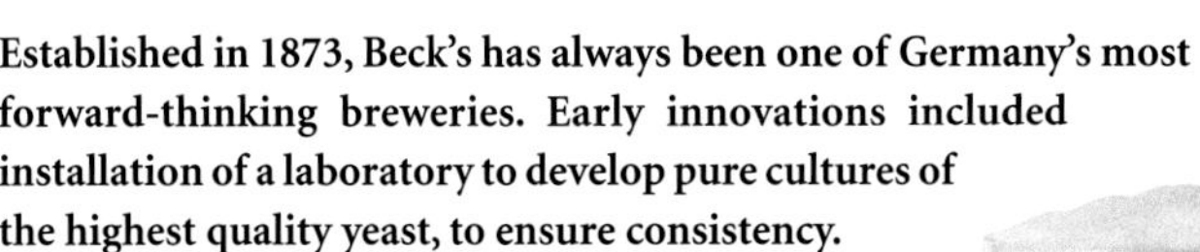

Established in 1873, Beck's has always been one of Germany's most forward-thinking breweries. Early innovations included installation of a laboratory to develop pure cultures of the highest quality yeast, to ensure consistency.

Another vital component in Beck's success story was the fact that its light, bottom-fermented beers were designed to travel well. Today, Beck's is Germany's most exported beer. Also, while other breweries allow their beers to be brewed under licence in other countries, every single bottle of Beck's is produced at the Bremen brewery in accordance with the Reinheitsgebot purity laws. The standard pilsener, the original Beck's beer, is a crisp and dry – very much a thirst-quenching drink.

SPECIFICATIONS
Brewery: Brauerei Beck
Location: Bremen
Style: Pilsener
Colour: Pale golden yellow
Alcohol: 5%
Serving temperature: 8°C (46.4°F)
Food: All kinds of fish

Berliner Kindl Weisse

When Berlin became capital of Germany in the late nineteenth century it went through a period of massive growth in both population and industry.

It was during this period, in 1870, that the Berliner Kindl brewery was established. The brewery started producing its pilsener in 1896, after it acquired the Potsdam brewery which specialized in the new style of bottom-fermented beer. Its wheat beer is of a characteristically northern style, which, unlike the wheat beers of the south, is brewed with lactic acid giving it a sour lemony flavour reminiscent of Champagne. The low alcohol content makes it a refreshing summer drink.

SPECIFICATIONS

Brewery: Berliner Kindl Brauerei
Location: Berlin, Brandenburg, eastern Germany
Style: Berliner Weissbier
Colour: Pale yellow
Alcohol: 2.7%
Serving temperature: 8°–10°C (46.4°–50°F)
Food: Roast pork or chicken

Clausthaler Non-alcoholic

The strict Reinheitsgebot purity laws of Germany mean that no beer may be made with any ingredients other than water, malt, hops and yeast.

However, while they specify what may go into a beer, they make no restriction on what may be taken out. Launched in 1979, Clausthaler was developed by the Binding brewery using a pioneering technique called 'arrested fermentation' to brew an authentic beer, but without the alcohol (the 0.5% alcohol is within the permitted definition for non-alcoholic beer and is lower than the alcohol content of some breads). And although it lacks alcohol, it does not lack flavour, having a light but pleasantly floral hoppy character.

SPECIFICATIONS

Brewery: Binding Brauerei
Location: Frankfurt
Style: Lager
Colour: Pale golden yellow
Alcohol: 0.5%
Serving temperature: 8°C (46.4°F)
Food: Light flavoured soups and pasta dishes

Binding Römer Pilsener

This full-flavoured pilsener beer was launched in 1939 by the Binding brewery of Frankfurt and is named after the ancient city hall. An authentic classic pilsener, it has a crisp, refreshing flavour with a herby, spicy hop character, leading to a dry, bitter hop finish.

Römer is also available in a premium version called Römer Pilsener Spezial. The extensive Binding range also includes a full-flavoured malty Export, a dark, fruity altbier called Kutscher Alt, and a strong, dark double bock with a complex fruity flavour, called Carolus der Starke, named after Karl the Great, one of the founders of Frankfurt. The Binding label bears the classic eagle emblem of the city of Frankfurt, and the beer is the defining pilsener of both the city and the region. Other Binding products include BBK Marzen, Binding Black Lager, Binding Export and Binding Ice.

SPECIFICATIONS
Brewery: Binding Brauerei
Location: Frankfurt
Style: Pilsener
Colour: Golden yellow
Alcohol: 4.9%
Serving temperature: 8°C (46.4°F)
Food: An appetising beer to drink by itself as an aperitif

Schöfferhofer Hefeweizen

Binding is one of the largest brewing groups in Germany, based in Frankfurt, where it was founded in 1870. In 1921 it merged with two other breweries, Frankfurter Bürgerbrauerei and Hofbierbrauerei Schöfferhof to form Schöfferhof-Binding-Bürgerbräu AG.

The Schöfferhofer label is used as the brand for the brewery's range of Bavarian-style wheat beers, principal of which is Hefeweizen. This sparkling unfiltered beer has a potent fruity aroma and flavour characterized by apples, orange zest and hints of banana, with underlying spiciness reminiscent of cloves, and a touch of hoppy bite in the finish. Others in the range include a Dunkelweizen (dark wheat beer) and a filtered Kristallweizen.

SPECIFICATIONS
Brewery: Binding Brauerei
Location: Frankfurt
Style: Hefe-Weizen
Colour: Cloudy golden yellow
Alcohol: 5%
Serving temperature: 8°–10° C (46.4°–50°F)
Food: A crisp green salad

Bitburger Premium

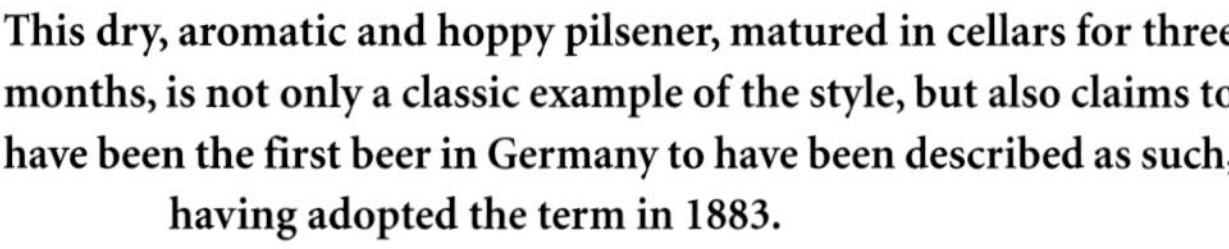

This dry, aromatic and hoppy pilsener, matured in cellars for three months, is not only a classic example of the style, but also claims to have been the first beer in Germany to have been described as such, having adopted the term in 1883.

The brewery itself was established in 1817 by local brewer and landlord Johan Peter Wallenborn, but it was one of his descendants, Theobald Simon, who built 'lagering' cellars that allowed the brewery to produce bottom-fermented beers that would keep well throughout the warm summer months. Today, Bitburger Premium Pils is one of the best-selling pilseners in Germany. Bitburger also produces the famous Köstritzer Schwarzbier, a classic black beer of the Thuringia region that dates back to the sixteenth century.

SPECIFICATIONS

Brewery: Bitburger Brauerei
Location: Bitburg, Rhineland-Palatinate
Style: Pilsener
Colour: Golden
Alcohol: 4.8%
Serving temperature: 8°–9°C (46.4°–48.2°F)
Food: A fine aperitif to stimulate the appetite

DAB Original

In the nineteenth century, Dortmund had a large coal and steel industry. All the local breweries produced a full-flavoured malty style of bottom-fermenting beer to quench workers' thirst.

These beers were slightly darker and slightly less hoppy than a typical pilsener. Dortmund's beers were soon popular well outside the local area, even as far afield as Japan. It is for this reason that the style came to be known as 'export', although it is also referred to as Dortmunder. Founded in 1868, Dortmunder Aktien Brauerei was one of the city's original producers of the style and remains a leading exponent, brewing DAB to the original recipe.

SPECIFICATIONS

Brewery: Dortmunder Actien Brauerei
Location: Dortmund, North Rhine-Westphalia
Style: Dortmunder / export
Colour: Crystal-clear golden yellow
Alcohol: 4.8%
Serving temperature: 6°–8°C (42.8°–46.4°F)
Food: Cold meat and cheese platters

Diebels Alt

The deep copper hues and rich malty, hoppy aromas of this top-fermented ale mark it out as a classic of the altbier ('old beer') style.

Diebels Alt is a beer with plenty of body, filling the mouth satisfyingly and yet feeling light and effervescent. The flavour is refreshingly dry and bitter, with aggressive Perle and Hallertau hops dominating the gentle sweetness of dark malt that gives an underlying taste of brown sugar (the husks of the malt are removed to reduce the characteristic 'burnt' taste). The brewery was founded in 1878 by Josef Diebels, in the picturesque village of Issum in the Niederrhein region, close to the Dutch border and not far from Düsseldorf, an area that is strongly associated with altbiers and home to most of its finest examples.

SPECIFICATIONS
Brewery: Privatbrauerei Diebel
Location: Issum am Niederrhein, Rhineland
Style: Altbier
Colour: Bright, clear copper
Alcohol: 4.8%
Serving temperature: 9°–10°C (48.2°–50°F)
Food: Weisswurst and sauerkraut

Erdinger Weissbier

Erdinger proudly claims to be the world's biggest wheat beer brewer and is also one of the oldest. Founded in 1886 by a local man, Johann Kienle, it was taken over by Franz Brombach in 1935 and has been run by his son Werner since 1975.

Unfiltered, bottle-conditioned Erdinger Weissbier remains the brewery's flagship product and is a classic Bavarian wheat beer, with a sweet, malty flavour and a slight hop bitterness. The brewery's range takes in seven other varieties, including a clear, fine-filtered Kristallweiss, a traditional dark version with a rich, smooth and slightly spicy flavour, and a strong, dark bock beer which has an extra-long maturing period.

SPECIFICATIONS
Brewery: Erdinger Weissbräu
Location: Erding, Bavaria
Style: Hefe-Weizen / Weissbier
Colour: Cloudy pale yellow
Alcohol: 5.3%
Serving temperature: 10°–12°C (50°–53.6°F)
Food: Serve as an apéritif

Früh Kölsch

This beer pours a nice light golden amber with a small white head. The aromas are a blend of malt and bread, with a slight hoplike spice, and perhaps a hint of berries.

The taste is very refreshing, perfectly balanced, with the nice crisp malts dominating the flavour. A slight fruit and hop bitterness is barely noticeable, but complements the style perfectly. The beer has a nice light body and is very drinkable. Kölsch is an appellation applied to top-fermented beers brewed only in Cologne.

SPECIFICATIONS
Brewery: Brauerei P.J. Früh
Location: Cologne, North Rhine-Westphalia
Style: Kölsch
Colour: Pale lemon gold
Alcohol: 4.8%
Serving temperature: 5°C (41°F)
Food: Wurst, rye bread

Hannen Alt

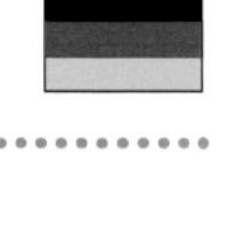

Part of the Danish brewing group Carlsberg since 1988, Hannen was founded in 1725 and its classic Altbier (old beer) is still brewed at the original site in Mönchengladbach, near Düsseldorf.

Altbier is a particular speciality of this region. It is a copper-coloured top-fermenting ale that spends a long period maturing in cold storage and gets its name from the fact that the style pre-dates the more modern pilsener. Hannen's version has a smooth, creamy body and an earthy, dark fruit character in the aroma and on the palate, with moderate herbal hop bitterness in the finish. Hannen also brews Carlsberg beers in Germany.

SPECIFICATIONS
Brewery: Hannen Brauerei GmBH
Location: Mönchengladbach, North Rhine-Westphalia
Style: Altbier
Colour: Dark copper-red
Alcohol: 4.8%
Serving temperature: 6°–8°C (42.8°–46.4°F)
Food: Hamburgers or sausages

Hasseröder Premium Pils

Hasseröder brewery was founded in 1872 in the ancient town of Wernigerode, a popular tourist spot which still has many half-timbered medieval houses and parts of the old city walls intact.

It was taken over by Ernst Schreyer in 1882, soon becoming one of Germany's major breweries. After many years hidden away behind the Iron Curtain, Hasseröder once again came to prominence following German reunification in 1990 and is one of the top five best-selling pilseners in the domestic market. The brewery produces just one beer, the same beer that it has always made, a rich, golden pilsener with a sweet, refreshing flavour.

SPECIFICATIONS

Brewery: Hasseröder Brauerei
Location: Wernigerode, Saxony-Anhalt
Style: Pilsener
Colour: Clear golden yellow
Alcohol: 4.8%
Serving temperature: 6°–8°C (42.8°–46.4°F)
Food: Fresh green salad

Jever Pilsener

The Friesisches Brauhaus at Jever, in northern Germany, produces this famous lager, and has a tradition going back 150 years.

This is probably the most bitter of the Nothern German pilseners. It has an aroma of resiny hops and booming malt leading to a beer with a typical pure white head and just the right amount of carbonation. The taste is of grassy, resiny hops held up well by a very supportive malt base. The label says 'Friesisch Herb', which means 'fresh, dry', and this is so. (The word 'herb' can also mean 'bitter', which is also applicable in this case.) The beer is bouncingly fresh, but dry from the high hop rate – although still with plenty of mouthfeel. It continues through in the same way to a refreshing, lasting, hop-filled finish.

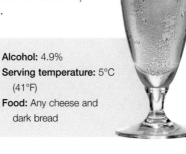

SPECIFICATIONS

Brewery: Friesisches Bauhaus
Location: Jever, Friesland
Style: Pilsener
Colour: Golden
Alcohol: 4.9%
Serving temperature: 5°C (41°F)
Food: Any cheese and dark bread

Kulmbacher Premium Pils

The Kulmbacher brewery group was formed from the merger of five independent breweries all based in the small town of Kulmbach, known as the 'capital city of beer'. Kulmbacher Premium Pils is its flagship beer, a straightforward lager with a light flavour.

Following the merger, beer production was moved to a single site, although many of the individual recipes were retained. The Kulmbacher label is applied to several famous brands, including Reichelbräu Eisbock 24, an ice-conditioned beer that was formerly a contender for the title of world's strongest beer.

SPECIFICATIONS
Brewery: Kulmbacher Brauerei
Location: Kulmbach, Franconia, Bavaria
Style: Pilsener

Colour: Pale straw yellow
Alcohol: 4.9%
Serving temperature: 6°–8°C (42.8°–46.4°F)
Food: Summer salads

Löwenbräu

Some sources date the formation of Löwenbräu (the Lion brewery) to 1383, but this view is not without controversy.

Löwenbräu was bought by Georg Brey in 1818, and under his direction it grew to become the biggest brewery in Munich, eventually merging with Spaten in 1997. Löwenbräu Original is a classic Munich lager, soft and malty with a light hoppy background. The brewery's range also includes a dry, hoppy Premium Pilsener, a non-alcoholic beer, and a golden unfiltered Bavarian wheat beer, as well as its annual seasonal speciality strong beer for the world-famous Munich Oktoberfest.

SPECIFICATIONS
Brewery: Löwenbräu AG
Location: Munich
Style: Munich light lager

Colour: Golden yellow
Alcohol: 5.2%
Serving temperature: 8°C (46.4°F)
Food: Chinese noodle dishes

Paulaner Hefe-Weissbier

The city of Munich was given its name in 1158 by Duke Henry the Lion and is derived from an old German word meaning 'Monks' Place', reflecting the fact that since the eighth century the area has been the site of many monastic communities.

The Paulaner monastery was founded on a hillside by followers of St Francis of Paula in the sixteenth century. Like all monasteries it took up brewing early on; the surplus was sold to local bars for public consumption. The first official document detailing the existence of the Paulaner brewery dates from 1634. Traditionally known for its lagers, in recent years it has concentrated its efforts towards a popular range of wheat beers. The classic unfiltered golden Hefe-Weizbier has a spicy clove aroma and a crisp, refreshing fruity flavour.

SPECIFICATIONS
Brewery: Paulaner GmbH
Location: Munich, Bavaria
Style: Hefe-Weizen / Weissbier
Colour: Golden orange-yellow

Alcohol: 5.5%
Serving temperature: 9°–12°C (48.2°–53.6°F)
Food: Chicken and vegetable pie

Rostocker Pilsener

Rostocker Pilsener is a light, refreshing golden beer with a pronounced hoppy dryness. It comes from the historic Hanseatic Brewery of Rostock, which can trace its origins back to 1258.

The brewery was already a well-established exporter of beers by 1878, when it was taken over by Georg Mahn and Friedrich Ohlerich. Its fortunes really took off, with the establishment of its own maltings and refrigeration plant. During World War II, the brewery was dismantled by Soviet troops, but amazingly it recovered from this setback and was brewing once again by 1947. It now produces a range of four beers, including light and dark bocks and a strong 'export'.

SPECIFICATIONS
Brewery: Rostocker Brauerei
Location: Rostock, Schleswig-Holstein
Style: Pilsener
Colour: Golden yellow

Alcohol: 4.9%
Serving temperature: 6°–8°C (42.8°–46.4°F)
Food: Curried rice dishes

Franziskaner

The name 'Franziskaner' relates to the Franciscan monastery that stood across the street from the old wheat beer brewery in the centre of Munich.

The existence of the brewery was first recorded in 1363, when it was the Seidel Vaterstetter brewery. The two regular Franziskaner brews – Helles (light) and Dunkel (dark) – are both traditional unfiltered top-fermented wheat beers full of flavour. Wheat beers generally tend to be brewed with around 50% wheat and 50% malted barley, but unusually Franziskaner beers are brewed with 75% malted wheat. Helles has a light fruity, spicy aroma with a hint of cloves and bananas; the Dunkel has a richer, fuller flavour with a creamy malt character and chocolate notes.

SPECIFICATIONS

Brewery: Spaten-Franziskaner-Bräu
Location: Munich, Bavaria
Style: Hefe-Weizen / Weissbier
Colour: Pale golden yellow
Alcohol: 5%
Serving temperature: 10°–12°C (50°–53.6°F)
Food: Lightly flavoured chicken

Spaten Original Munich

Spaten was the first brewery in Munich to brew a pilsener-style lager, which it launched in 1894 with the intention of exporting it to northern Germany, but it was soon made available to the local market. This is the same beer sold today as Spaten Original Munich.

It has a delicately spicy aroma and a refreshing, light-bodied, mild flavour. Although its flagship beer is of such recent origin, the brewery is much older, dating back to 1397 when Hans Welser founded the Welser Prew brewery in Munich's Neuhausergasse. Over the next 125 years the brewery changed hands many times, before it entered a time of relative stability and acquired the name Spaten. In 1997, having celebrated its 600th anniversary, the brewery merged with Löwenbräu.

SPECIFICATIONS

Brewery: Spaten-Franziskaner-Bräu
Location: Munich, Bavaria
Style: Pilsener
Colour: Clear golden yellow
Alcohol: 5.2%
Serving temperature: 6°–8°C (42.8°–46.4°F)
Food: Smoked salmon quiche

Weihenstephaner Hefe-Weissbier

Reputedly the oldest brewery in the world, Weihenstephan is located in the university town of Freising, close to Munich.

It was founded in 1040 as the monastery brewery for the Benedictine monks. Over the years the monastery burned down four times and was ravaged on numerous other occasions by plagues, famines, wars and an earthquake. It was dissolved in 1803 and ownership passed over to the Bavarian state, but the brewery still stands on the same site on top of the Weihenstephan hill. While being of the most traditional breweries in the world, it is also one of the most modern, with state-of-the-art technology in its brewing facilities. Today it produces a wide range of beers, including a mild-flavoured pale lager and a full-flavoured Hefe-Weissbier.

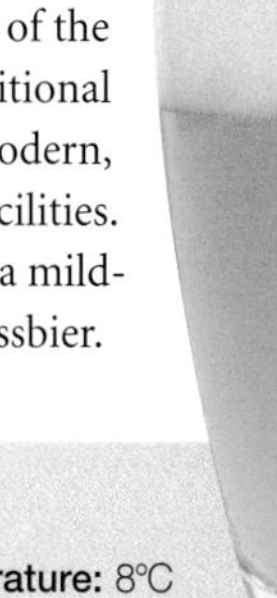

SPECIFICATIONS

Brewery: Brauerei Weihenstephan
Location: Freising
Style: Munich Helles lager
Colour: Pale yellow
Alcohol: 5.1%
Serving temperature: 8°C (46.4°F)
Food: Rich, earthy soups and stews

Warsteiner Premium Verum

Warsteiner was founded more than 250 years ago and in many ways is a deeply traditional brewery, producing all of its beers in accordance with Germany's ancient Reinheitsgebot purity laws.

Yet it also accommodates modern trends by presenting its classic pilsener in a slim, long-necked bottle to suit those people who prefer to drink from the bottle rather than a glass. Premium Verum is an authentic pilsener with a fragrant herbal hop aroma and a refreshingly dry, bitter flavour. It is available in versions flavoured with cola, lemon and orange, as well as an alcohol-free one. The Warsteiner brewery has sporting connections, sponsoring several prominent German football teams.

SPECIFICATIONS

Brewery: Warsteiner Brauerei
Location: Warstein, North Rhine-Westphalia
Style: Pilsener
Colour: Golden yellow
Alcohol: 4.8%
Serving temperature: 7°–8°C (44.6°–46.4°F)
Food: A stand-alone drink

Birra Cystall
alla spina-vom Fass
LAUTERBACHER
Maisel's Weisse

Italian Beers

Italy is predominantly a wine-producing country and ranks low among European countries for beer consumption. Still, certain areas of the country, particularly the north, have a strong brewing tradition, stemming from the Austrian influence exerted when the northern kingdoms of Italy were part of the mighty Hapsburg empire.

The Lombardy and Veneto regions in particular saw a steady influx of Austrian merchants and businessmen who settled there and brought with them their native customs. But brewing remained a small-scale domestic activity until 1829, when Italy's first commercial brewery was established in Brescia by an Austrian, Peter Wührer. The dominant style of beer to this day is a typically Austrian easy-drinking malty golden lager.

By the end of the nineteenth century, there were around 100 commercial breweries in Italy. Then in the twentieth century large companies such as Peroni expanded, absorbing many smaller regional breweries and concentrating the brewing industry. By the 1980s, most major European brewers had entered the Italian market, with the Dutch giant Heineken in particular establishing dominance over the domestic market. Carlsberg of Denmark bought Poretti, and Peroni established links with Kronenbourg of France.

While consumption is still relatively low, in recent years beer has become fashionable with younger Italians. Microbreweries such as Le Baladin produce and sell more interesting artisanal products, and imported beers from England and Germany are finding favour. Organizations such as the Slow Food movement are also having a positive influence.

Left: Italian wines are known the world over, but with the international spread of beers such as Peroni Italian skills in beer producing are steadily becoming recognized as well. The Italian brewers excel in making clean, classic pale lagers which are ideal for the easy-drinking café-bar lifestyle enjoyed by many Italian locals and visitors to Italy alike.

STATISTICS

Total production: 13,672,000 hectolitres (361,176,000 gallons) per year

Consumption per capita: 29 litres (8 gallons) per year

Famous breweries: Birra Peroni Industriale; Castello di Udine; Dreher; Pedavena; Spezialbier-Brauerei Forst; Theresianer Alte Brauerei Triest

Famous brands: Birra Moretti la Rossa; Dreher; Forst Kronen; Pedavena; Peroni Gran Reserva

Above: While wine may still predominate as the drink of choice for Italians, beer is quickly gaining in popularity among the younger and more style-conscious.

Le Baladin Super

Super was the first beer created by Le Baladin ('The Troubadour') when owner Teo Musso Materino began brewing at his historic pub in the village of Piozzo in 1996.

Materino learned the craft of brewing in Belgium, and Super is a top-fermented *doppio malto* (double malt) ale inspired by Belgian abbey beers. It is characterized by an intense floral aroma with apricot, ripe banana and bitter almond notes, and has a well-balanced flavour with hints of apricot and citrus fruits. It was awarded the title of Best Italian Ale on its first appearance at the Great British Beer Festival in 2000. Le Baladin also produces a range of products called Kikke Baladin, made from its beers, including a beer jelly to serve with cheeses and cold meats.

SPECIFICATIONS
Brewery: Le Baladin
Location: Piozzo, Piedmont
Style: Belgian abbey double
Colour: Amber
Alcohol: 8%
Serving temperature: 10°–12°C (50°–53.6°F)
Food: Cheeses and pastries

Peroni Gran Riserva

The award-winning Peroni Gran Riserva was launched in 1996 to mark the 150th anniversary of the Peroni brewery.

Presented in an elegant bottle with a gilt label bearing the picture of the brewery's founder, Giovanni Peroni, it is reputedly based on a recipe devised by Peroni himself. It is classified as a *doppio malto* (double malt) beer, brewed broadly in the style of a German Maibock, although Peroni's version is available all year round. It is made using exclusively pilsener malts, which give the beer its characteristic deep golden colour, and is brewed using the complex double decoction mash process, before being aromatized with Saaz hops, then matured for two months. The finished product is a well-rounded, delicately balanced beer.

SPECIFICATIONS
Brewery: Birra Peroni Industriale
Location: Rome, Lazio
Style: Maibock
Colour: Deep golden yellow
Alcohol: 6.6%
Serving temperature: 9°C (48.2°F)
Food: Savoury pork dishes, soft cheeses

Birra Moretti La Rossa

One of the most characterful beers from Italy, Moretti La Rossa is named for its ruby red hues, which arise from the use of Vienna malt, so called after the distinctive style of beers that became popular in that city in the nineteenth century.

It is actually classified as a *doppio malto* (double malt) beer, brewed in the style of a German double bock. La Rossa has a rich, sweet aroma with notes of caramel and toffee, a thick, creamy texture and a full, robust flavour with a sweet, buttery caramel malt character tempered by hints of bitter chocolate. La Rossa was originally brewed by Moretti, established by Luigi Moretti in 1859 in the city of Friuli, north of Venice. It is now part of the Heineken group, and was renamed Castello di Udine.

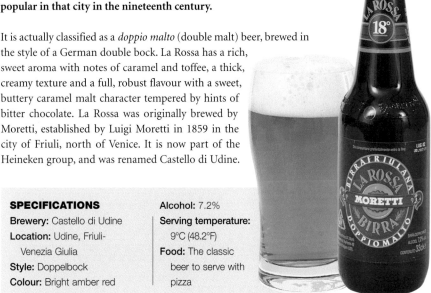

SPECIFICATIONS
Brewery: Castello di Udine
Location: Udine, Friuli-Venezia Giulia
Style: Doppelbock
Colour: Bright amber red
Alcohol: 7.2%
Serving temperature: 9°C (48.2°F)
Food: The classic beer to serve with pizza

Dreher

The first Dreher brewery was founded in Vienna in 1773 by Franz Anton Dreher, who was a member of a Bohemian family that had been brewing since the seventeenth century.

The company expanded to Italy in 1865, opening a brewery in Trieste in the north of the country. In 1974 it was taken over by the Dutch brewing group Heineken, becoming the first piece in the Heineken Italia jigsaw. Its flagship beer is a classic golden lager with a light hoppy aroma and a smooth, well-balanced flavour with a dry, slightly bitter character.

SPECIFICATIONS
Brewery: Dreher
Location: Milan, Lombardy
Style: Lager
Colour: Golden yellow
Alcohol: 4.7%
Serving temperature: 5°–7°C (41°–44.6°F)
Food: Chicken and mozzarella salad

Menabrea 150 Anniversario

First brewed in 1996 to celebrate the 150th anniversary of the brewery, this is a straightforward easy-drinking lager with a well-balanced flavour of malt and hops.

Italy's oldest brewery, Menabrea was founded in 1846 by the brothers Gian Battista and Antonio Caraccio, who then sold it in 1854 to Jean Joseph Menabrea and Anton Zimmerman. The pair were already partners in the Zimmerman brewery in Aosta; by 1872 Zimmerman had returned to Aosta, leaving the partnership in the hands of Menabrea and his sons, since when it has gone on to win numerous international awards for its beers.

SPECIFICATIONS

Brewery: Menabrea
Location: Biella, Piedmont
Style: Lager
Colour: Deep golden yellow
Alcohol: 4.8%
Serving temperature: 6°–8°C (42.8°–46.4°F)
Food: White meats and light-flavoured cheeses

Pedavena

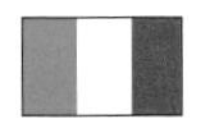

This golden pilsener was first brewed by the Pedavena brewery in 1897, the year the brewery was established by the Luciani family.

It is a well-balanced beer with a fine hop aroma and a delicate hop bitterness on the palate. Located in the town of Trento, Pedavena brewery is named after the picturesque region north of Verona in the foothills of the Dolomite mountains. Since the mid-1970s, Pedavena has been part of the Dutch-owned Heineken Italia brewing group. The brewery also produces a refreshing, full-flavoured amber-coloured Bavarian-style 'Weizen' (wheat beer), as well as various seasonal and special-occasion beers.

SPECIFICATIONS

Brewery: Pedavena
Location: Trento, Trentino-Alto Adige
Style: Pilsener
Colour: Deep golden yellow
Alcohol: 5%
Serving temperature: 4°–6°C (39.2°–42.8°F)
Food: Grilled tuna steaks

Forst Kronen

The village of Lagundo lies to the west of Merano in the mountainous Alto Adige (southern Tirol) region of the far north of Italy, an area that has historically been influenced very strongly by neighbouring Austria.

This influence is notably apparent in the beers of the Forst brewery, which derives its name from the German for 'forest' and is owned by the Fuchs family, who are of Austrian descent. Forst Kronen (Kronen being from the German for 'crown') is characteristic of the typical golden style of lager popular in Vienna, with a rich, malty flavour and a light use of hops to provide balance and a refreshingly dry, gently bitter finish.

SPECIFICATIONS

Brewery: Spezialbier-Brauerei Forst
Location: Lagundo, Trentino-Alto Adige
Style: Lager
Colour: Golden yellow
Alcohol: 5.2%
Serving temperature: 8°C (46.4°F)
Food: Smoked sausages and cured meats

Theresianer Vienna

This classic red Vienna-style lager has been brewed in Trieste since the start of the twentieth century. It has a smooth, easy-drinking character with a mild flavour that carefully balances malt and hops.

The Theresianer brewery produces a wide range of traditional beer styles, including a classic bottom-fermented golden pilsener, a Bavarian-style Weizen (wheat beer) and a strong amber ale with a potent hop flavour. The symbol of the brewery, depicted on the labels of the bottles, is the Barbour lighthouse, which is also the symbol of the city of Trieste where the brewery was originally based, although it has now moved to new premises in nearby Treviso.

SPECIFICATIONS

Brewery: Theresianer Alte Brauerei Triest
Location: Treviso, Veneto
Style: Vienna lager
Colour: Copper red
Alcohol: 5.3%
Serving temperature: 8°C (46.4°F)
Food: Chocolate-based desserts

BÜRGERBRÄU
KAISER
BIER
INNSBRUCK

Austrian Beers

Beers are brewed in Austria in a wide range of styles and with a good deal of skill and care. The country has nearly 70 brewing concerns, including a few microbreweries and several brewpubs. While still to undergo the sort of new brewery revolution under way in the United States and the United Kingdom, the trend is still encouraging.

The greatest concentration of breweries is in Oberösterreich, which has almost a third of the total. It borders Bavaria and has many historical and cultural links with this region, and as a consequence it is here that the strongest Austrian beer tradition is to be found. In the eastern and southern parts of the country there are fewer producers, and they tend to be larger and more industrial in character – although both Vienna and Graz have recently established brewpubs.

The wide range of styles of beer encompasses most of those from South Germany, although often with subtle differences. There are also a couple which are specific to Austria, although there are no real examples of the classic Vienna amber lager, developed by Anton Dreher in the nineteenth century. Beers are only considered full-strength if brewed to at least 12° plato (a measure of specific gravity, relating to the amount of mashed barley in the wort). Average beer strengths must be among the highest in the world, with almost nothing under 5% and beers of more than 4% labelled as 'leicht', or light.

Austrian beer has long played second fiddle to German beer in terms of reputation. This is unfair, and many Austrian beers are more than capable of competing with those across the border in terms of quality. While strong pale lagers are certainly popular, there are many other more idiosyncratic Austrian styles such the unfiltered Keller or Zwickl beers.

Left: Kaiser Bier is Austria's best-selling lager, and is a fairly typical light pilsener of 5% abv. Although Kaiser's alcohol content is similar to mainstream European lagers, many Austrian beers are formidably powerful, typically ranging from 7% to 12% abv and beyond.

Above: In every tent at an Austrian beer festival you will find very strong men or women carrying steins of beer, which can contain up to 3 litres (5 pints).

STATISTICS

Total production: 8,891,000 hectolitres (234,875,000 gallons) per year

Consumption per capita: 107 litres (28 gallons) per year

Famous breweries: Braü Union Österreich; Brauerei Schwechat; Brauerei Zipfer; Hirter Brauerei; Ottakringer

Famous brands: Goldfassl Pils; Hirter Privat Pils; Kaiser; Schwechater Zwickl

Schloss Eggenberg Hopfenkönig

Hopfenkönig is claimed to be Schloss Eggenberg's most successful beer on the Austrian market. An excellent pilsener, it is brewed with the world-famous Saazer hops.

Matured slowly and highly fermented, it is brewed with only natural ingredients that conform to a German purity law dating back to 1516. The taste is full-bodied with a dry hoppiness and a good deal of rich and fruity malt. There is bitterness, but it is not very powerful. It has a thick bread-like taste reminiscent of German malts. The aftertaste is malty and a little roasted, with a honey-like sweetness and aromatic hops. The carbonation is fine, with some microscopic bubbles. The magnificent château Schloss Eggenberg is situated on the western outskirts of Graz. It has been in the possession of the Forstinger-Stöhr family for more than 200 years, and beer has been brewed there since the fourteenth century. Commercial production began in 1681.

SPECIFICATIONS

Brewery: Schloss Eggenberg
Location: Vorchdorf
Style: Pilsener
Colour: Gold

Alcohol: 5.1%
Serving temperature: 6°–8°C (43°–46°F)
Food: Serve as an apéritif with canapés

Hirter Privat Pils

Hirter brewery in Austria's Karnten region, close to the castle city of Friesach, claims to be able to trace its origins all the way back to 1270, when it was the house brewery for the Taverna Ze Hurde in the small town of Hirt; the Braükeller bar still operates today.

Hirter beers are brewed according to traditional methods and never pasteurized, instead using cold filtration to purify the end product. The brewery's flagship beer is its Privat Pils, produced according to an old Bohemian recipe and matured for a lengthy period to give it a smooth, well-rounded flavour with a subtle but distinct hop character. Hirter also produces a wide range of other beer styles, including Morchl, a dark beer, Hirter 1270, an old-fashioned copper-coloured ale, and a naturally cloudy golden Weizen (wheat beer).

SPECIFICATIONS

Brewery: Hirter Brauerei
Location: Hirt, Karnten
Style: Pilsener
Colour: Golden

Alcohol: 5.2%
Serving temperature: 8°C (46.4°F)
Food: Spiced lamb meatballs

Kaiser Draught

Austria's largest brewing group started out in 1921 with the foundation of the Braubank AG, formed by the merger of several smaller regional breweries.

The group continued to grow throughout the twentieth century by acquiring other breweries across Austria, so that today its beers account for around 33% of the Austrian domestic beer-drinking market. The group's flagship product is Kaiser Draught, the number-one-selling beer in Austria. It is a golden lager with a fruity aroma, hints of orange and a well-balanced flavour that starts off predominantly sweet and malty, but has a long dry bitter hop finish.

SPECIFICATIONS

Brewery: Braü Union Österreich
Location: Linz
Style: Lager
Colour: Golden yellow

Alcohol: 5%
Serving temperature: 7°–9°C (44.6°–48.2°F)
Food: Grilled swordfish or tuna steaks

Ottakringer Goldfassl Pils

Today, Ottakringer maintains an identity as Vienna's local brewer and is its largest remaining independent beer-producing business.

Goldfassl Pils is a light, easy-drinking beer with a fresh, floral hop aroma and a well-balanced malt flavour. The brewery also produces another stronger beer under the Goldfassl label, called Goldfassl Spezial, with a full malty flavour leading to an increasingly dry, bitter finish. The brewery's standard range of beers under the Ottakringer label include Helles, a pale Munich-style Märzen lager with a delicate, well-balanced flavour, and Dunkles, a traditional dark Vienna lager with a distinctive reddish colour and a soft, malty flavour.

SPECIFICATIONS

Brewery: Ottakringer
Location: Vienna
Style: Pilsener
Colour: Deep golden yellow

Alcohol: 4.6%
Serving temperature: 9°C (48.2°F)
Food: Roast chicken or pork

Puntigamer Almradler

This very pleasant fruit beer pours a pale golden colour, with a creamy white head. The name 'Radler' means 'cyclist' and indicates the low alcohol content of the beer.

It is sweet, but not overpoweringly so, and there is a good flavour of hops. Half of this brew consists of Almdudler, which is a blend of water, sugar and herb essences. It is stored in oak barrels, where it develops its characteristic flavour. The other half consists of Puntigamer beer. This is a very refreshing drink, and much nicer than most other fruit beers, which tend to be cloyingly sweet. The Puntigamer Brewery, situated in the ancient and beautiful Austrian town of Graz, also brews a range of pale, amber and dark lagers.

SPECIFICATIONS
Brewery: Puntigamer
Location: Graz
Style: Fruit beer (Radler)
Colour: Pale gold

Alcohol: 2.5%
Serving temperature: 6°–8°C (43°–46°F)
Food: Serve as a thirst-quencher

Stiegl Pils

This classic German pilsener is a fine, lively type of beer, with a bouquet produced by premium-quality Saaz hops to stimulate the senses. It pours the colour of straw, with a white head that rises a long way out of the glass.

The aroma is grassy with just a faint hint of hops. The taste is grassy, too. There is not a great deal of malt profile, and just a little hoppy bite at the end. The mouthfeel is crisp but a little on the fizzy side, caused by too much carbonation. The first record of a brewery in Stiegl dates from 1492, the year Columbus sailed to the New World, and beer has been brewed at the present facility since 1863.

SPECIFICATIONS
Brewery: Stiegl
Location: Salzburg
Style: Pilsener
Colour: Pale straw

Alcohol: 4.9%
Serving temperature: 6°–8°C (43°–46°F)
Food: Smoked meats

Schwechater Zwickl

Zwickl is unfiltered, unpasteurized beer, and the Schwechat version is a characteristically cloudy golden yellow with a smooth, easy-drinking flavour and a fresh hop aroma.

The Schwechat brewery also produces a traditional Vienna lager with a fruity malt character, and a beer called Hopfenperle. Schwechat is one of the oldest breweries in Austria and can trace its origins back more than 350 years to its foundation in 1632 as the Klein-Schwechat brewery. In 1760, an ambitious waiter from Vienna named Franz Anton Dreher bought the lease on the Ober-Lanzendorf brewery, adding a second brewery in 1782, then acquiring the Klein-Schwechat brewery in 1796. The brewery started producing a bottom-fermented lager in 1841, which later became known as Vienna lager.

SPECIFICATIONS
Brewery: Brauerei Schwechat
Location: Schwechat
Style: Zwickelbier
Colour: Golden yellow
Alcohol: 5.4%
Serving temperature: 8°C (46.4°F)
Food: Pasta, rice dishes, sandwiches

Zipfer Märzen

This is a pleasant golden beer that pours with a good, frothy head. The aroma is full of hops and the flavour is of sweet malt. Smooth and very drinkable, this is an excellent thirst-quencher. There is a nice bitter finish, although it is a little watery.

The Zipfer brewery dates back to 1858, when an enterprising Viennese stockbroker opened a spa in Zipf and built a small brewery as an added attraction. Although coming from a new brewery by Austrian standards, Zipfer beer still had to be aged and was stored in the naturally cool cellars dug deep into the hills behind the brewery. Later, in 1899, artificial cooling became available. Although the brewery installed the new technical innovation, the natural cooling process in the mountain caves proved superior.

SPECIFICATIONS
Brewery: Zipfer (Brau Union AG)
Location: Zipf
Style: Oktoberfest Märzen
Colour: Gold
Alcohol: 5.0%
Serving temperature: 6°–8°C (43°–46°F)
Food: Pastries, snacks

U TŘÍ ZLATÝCH
HVĚZD
U TŘÍ
ZLATÝCH HVĚZD
RESTAURANT

Czech Beers

A great deal has changed in the Czech brewing world since the collapse of the communist bloc. The industry has been completely transformed by brewery closures, new technology and foreign takeovers, and not all of these changes have turned out to be for the better.

Still, no one can deny that the quality of Czech-brewed lager is still arguably the highest in the world, and that the choice of styles is excellent. Even in a large city such as Prague, where there are several large local breweries, there is a good choice of beer from the whole of the republic. There has been criticism, however, that the quality of the Czech lagers has slipped since the industry became privatized and the old 'family' breweries were snapped up by big international concerns. In Prague, for instance, the three large breweries – Staropramen, Braník and Mestan – were in a single group, Prazské Pivovary, and had the same owner. In November 1996, when the owner increased its shareholding to 51%, that owner was the British firm Bass. When Bass decided to get out of brewing, the breweries passed to the Belgian multinational Interbrew.

The Czech brewing industry today draws upon the country's ancient traditions of beer making. Hops production in Bohemia is recorded as far back as AD 859, and the first Czech brewery was established at Cerhenice in 1118. The industry's strength grew rapidly and it became ever more important to the country's infrastructure – by the early sixteenth century some towns generated as much 80% of their municipal income from beer production. Moreover, export sales of both beer and prized Bohemian hops were booming by the end of the Middle Ages. The fortunes of Czech beer dipped during the devastating years of the Thirty Years War (1618–48), pulling back only in the nineteenth century. The twentieth century brought more war and the post-World War II communist takeover, and a decline in quality. Since communism's collapse in the late 1980s, Czech beer has undergone a resurgence, regaining its worldwide reputation for quality.

Left: Czech drinkers enjoy their beer in a pavement café. The Czech brewing industry went through some tough times in the twentieth century under the effects of two world wars and the communist takeover. In recent times, however, it has reclaimed its reputation for lagers of the highest quality, and the Czech Republic is now a huge beer exporter, as well as producing beers for domestic consumption.

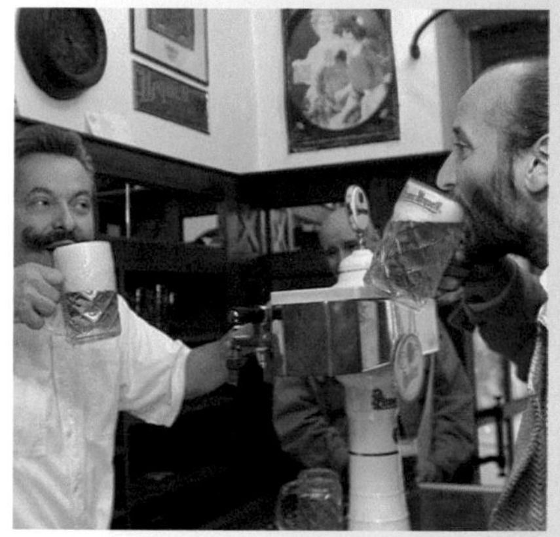

Above: Beer drinking could be classed as a national pastime in the Czech Republic, and the country's drinkers are passionate about the quality of their beers.

STATISTICS

Total production: 18,548,000 hectolitres (489,986,000 gallons) per year

Consumption per capita: 159 litres (42 gallons) per year

Famous breweries: Budejovicky Budvar; Pilsner Urquell; Pivovar U Fleku; Plzensky Prazdroj (SABMiller)

Famous brands: Budweiser Budvar; Eggengerb Kristián; Flekovsy Tmavy Lezák; Gambrinus Svetly Plvo

Budweiser Budvar

Budweiser Budvar, from the southern Czech town of Budejovice, is a strong golden lager with a light, smooth flavour that has more of a malty character than the classic pilseners from the town of Pilsen in the country's north. It is brewed using Saaz hops, Moravian barley malt and water from the brewery's artesian wells, and matured in traditional horizontal lagering tanks for at least 90 days.

Not to be confused with the Budweiser produced by the US brewer Anheuser-Busch, Budweiser Budvar takes its name from Budweis, the German form of Budejovice, the Budvar brewery's home town. A bitter dispute over rights to the name means that the Czech beer is called Czechvar in the United States, while the US beer is known in some European countries by its shortened form, Bud. There is some debate as to which is the 'original' Budweiser, but it seems perverse to prevent beer from Budejovice being called Budweiser.

SPECIFICATIONS
Brewery: Budejovicky Budvar
Location: Ceske Budejovice
Style: Lager
Colour: Golden amber-yellow
Alcohol: 5%
Serving temperature: 9°C (48°F)
Food: Roast beef and dumplings

Eggenberg Kristián

This type of beer is brewed in the classic Czech pale-lager style. Individual pilseners vary greatly, from sweetish and malty (such as Pilsner Urquell) to dry and hoppy (Budvar). One thing they all have in common is being heavily hopped with Saaz, a hop with a good aroma. Kristián is sweet, with a slight hops bitterness underneath.

Beer-brewing tradition in Cesky Krumlov dates back to 1336, when the citizens were granted a charter to make malt and brew and sell beer. In 1560 a new brewery was built that used high-quality water. In 1622 the Eggenberg family gained control of Krumlov; in 1625–30 the brewery relocated to its current building. Under the Schwarzenberg family (from 1719), the building was gradually refashioned in the Baroque style, and the brewery was updated.

SPECIFICATIONS
Brewery: Pivovar Eggenberg
Location: Cesky Krumlov
Style: Pilsener
Colour: Gold
Alcohol: 4.0%
Serving temperature: 6°–8°C (43°–46°F)
Food: Serve as an apéritif

Flekovsky Tmavy Lezák

Dark brown in colour, this dunkel pours with a decent finger-thick head and an aroma of roasted smoky malt. The flavours are of malt, dark chocolate, coffee and toffee. The aftertaste is a little sour. Available bottled and on draught, this beer is the only one brewed by Prague's famous beer hall and brewery, U Fleku, which is situated in the city centre.

It is said that the owners acquired the rights to brew beer there in the year 1499, but the ancient brewing house can be dated roughly to the year 1360. The beer, the dark Flekovsky lezák, licensed in 1499 to be brewed at U Fleku, is one of the oldest in Prague. The present name of the establishment dates from the eighteenth century. In 1762 a certain Jakub Flekovskych and his wife purchased it, and the pub was given the name U Flekovskych. The name has since been shortened.

SPECIFICATIONS
Brewery: Pivovar U Fleku
Location: Prague
Style: Dunkel
Colour: Dark brown
Alcohol: 4.6%
Serving temperature: 10°C (50°F)
Food: Sausages, cold meats

Gambrinus Svetle Pivo

One of the most popular lagers to be found in the Czech Republic, and for that matter in Eastern Europe, Gambrinus Svetle Pivo has an attractive malty aroma and a bitter flavour that sets it apart from other beers of similar style.

It pours well, with a creamy head and lacing that last for quite a long time, and is equally at home when served as an apéritif or at a party. It is available in both bottled and canned forms, the former probably being the most popular.

SPECIFICATIONS
Brewery: Plzensky Prazdroj (SABMiller)
Location: Plzen
Style: Pilsener
Colour: Yellow
Alcohol: 4.1%
Serving temperature: 43°–46°F (6°–8°C)
Food: Serve as an apéritif

Slovakian Beers

In medieval times, home brewing was banned in the villages of what was to become Slovakia, in favour of officially licensed breweries in towns, which were fed by the tithes serfs had to pay in hops and barley. Beer-loving serfs were forced to buy their brew from these regional monopolies.

This probably explains why beer for centuries came second place in the hearts of many Slovaks, to home distillates such as *slivovica* (plum brandy). With the creation of Czechoslovakia in 1918, the influence of the Bohemian style on Slovak beer was absolute. When the breweries nationalized after communism's post-war rise, the main technical school for budding brewers, and the one from which breweries recruited for their top positions, was in Prague.

For years the Slovak brewing industry lagged far behind that in the Czech heartland. The communists built several large, new breweries in the 1950s and 1960s in an attempt to rectify this situation; the five largest Slovak breweries in existence today are the result of this initiative. Closures among the independents have left Slovakia with only four breweries founded before 1950. The largest brewery is SABMiller, which owns Pivovar Saris.

In 2004 Slovakia joined the EU. This meant that Slovak producers of alcoholic drinks were faced with new competition, as the import duties for products imported from the EU were cancelled. Just as in the Czech Republic, this situation spelled bad news for independent breweries trying to do business with the rest of Europe. In the domestic beer market, however, Slovak beer brands are very popular and consumers are very loyal to their favourite brands. The only real competition comes from the Czech Republic.

Left: Bratislava Castle and the river Danube, here seen during a picturesque dusk. Slovakia's identity has been a turbulent one throughout pre- and post-war history, but the country has maintained some first-rate brewing skills. Ironically, incorporation into the EU is the biggest threat to traditional beers.

Above: A stream of bottles flows from the production line in the Saris Brewery. Saris, which is located in Velky Saris, northeastern Slovakia, is owned by SABMiller and produces a refreshing range of beers.

STATISTICS

Total production: 4,676,000 hectolitres (12,352,685 gallons) per year
Consumption per capita: 93 litres (24.5 gallons) per year
Famous breweries: Corgon; Popper; Saris
Famous brands: 16% Palatin; Svetly Leziak

Corgon Svetly Leziak

As with most Czech and Slovak pilseners, this beer is a little darker than international brews that attempt to imitate the style. The colour is a slightly hazy amber, and there is a tangy aroma of apples and bread. The apple lingers in the flavour, but hops also come through subtly and there is a light bitterness. The brew becomes a little sticky as it warms up, yet the mouthfeel is thin and watery.

Corgon was a mythical being with enormous powers. Svetly Leziak simply means 'light lager'. Nitra, where the brewery is based, is a city in western Slovakia, about 70 km (43 miles) northwest of Slovakia's capital, Bratislava. It is located on the river Nitra, a tributary of the river Danube, in the rich agricultural area of the Danubian Lowlands.

SPECIFICATIONS
Brewery: Pivovar Corgon (Heineken)
Location: Nitra, Slovakia
Style: Lager
Colour: Amber
Alcohol: 4.9%
Serving temperature: 6°–8°C (43°–46°F)
Food: Serve as an apéritif

Popper Svetlé Pivo

The Popper brewery (Pivovar Popper) in Bytca produces a range of beers that include the classic Slovak pilsener pictured here. Popper's brews also include a German-style dunkel, as well as dark lagers and a Bock.

Palatin 16% is the strongest of the Popper beers, and is certainly the most satisfying from the body point of view. A good drink for late at night, it has an excellent relaxing effect. The flavour of this dark lager is sweet, with a taste of plums. The head is light brown, and leaves a fair amount of lacing on the glass. It has a light roasted bitterness and a medium body. The finish is reminiscent of a light cola, with a little stickiness.

SPECIFICATIONS
Brewery: Pivovar Popper
Location: Bytca, Slovakia
Style: Lager
Colour: Amber
Alcohol: 5.0%
Serving temperature: 6°–8°C (43°–46°F)
Food: Fried potatoes

Saris Premium

This is an undemanding, refreshing pilsener. It pours an attractive golden colour with a large white bubbly head that dissipates quickly. It has aromas of grain and flour, and some hops. The pleasant flavour is malty and grassy with a good tang and a slight buttery taste. There is good carbonation at the start. This is a rich brew with a lasting hoppy mouthfeel.

Velky Saris, where the brewery is located, is in northeastern Slovakia and is the administrative centre of the former province of Saris. One of the principal tourist attractions is a ruined twelfth-century castle. There is also a Gothic chapel dating from the middle of the fourteenth century.

SPECIFICATIONS
Brewery: Pivovar Saris (SABMiller)
Location: Velky Saris, Slovakia
Style: Pilsener
Colour: Gold
Alcohol: 4.6%
Serving temperature: 6°–8°C (43°–46°F)
Food: Drink as an apéritif or with snacks

Steiger 1% Tmavé

This dark beer pours with a small head and, for a low-alcohol brew, is very sweet. It has a full flavour with a strong taste of liquorice, and also a warming richness with an underlying characteristic of baked apples.

The 'Big Three' – Heineken, Saris and Topvar – capture 86% of the total market share of Slovakian brewing and are the largest breweries in Slovakia. The rest of the market belongs to small breweries – those that produce less than 200,000 hectolitres (5,290,000 gallons) of beer, such as Steiger, Stein, Tatrab and Popper. Along with the other small Slovak beweries, Steiger has been hard hit by the increased taxation imposed in 2003. Three breweries and two malt producers have shut down since then, and there has been an average annual decrease of 15% in beer sales.

SPECIFICATIONS
Brewery: Pivovar Steiger
Location: Vyhice, Slovakia
Style: Dunkel
Colour: Dark brown
Alcohol: 4.0%
Serving temperature: 10°C (50°F)
Food: Smoked meats, bread and cheese

Hungarian Beers

Peter Schmidt established the first commercial brewery in Hungary in Budapest in 1845. During the heyday of the Austro-Hungarian Empire, the Kobánya district of Budapest became the centre of Hungary's brewing industry. The Dreher Brewery was named after Anton Dreher (creator of the Vienna style of lager).

Dreher started a brewery in Budapest in 1862, and it went on to dominate the Hungarian market prior to World War II. Today, Hungary has only five large commercial brewers, which produce mainly lagers (Világos) and German-style dark beers (Barna). SABMiller now owns the Dreher (Kobánya) Brewery in Budapest. Its main products are the Dreher Classic and Arany Ászok, which are lagers brewed in the pilsener style, but it also brews Kobányai Világos, Dreher Lager and Dreher Bak. Dreher Bak is a double Bock, which is a very strong lager. Traditionally, it is brewed in the autumn and aged through the winter for consumption in the spring.

Interbrew owns 69% of the Borsod Brewery. In addition to the local brands of Borsodi Világos, Borsodi Barna, Borsodi Bivaly and Borostyán, it brews Stella Artois and Rolling Rock under licence. The Pécs Brewery is majority-owned by Ottakringer. Its brands are Pécsi Szalon, Szalon Barna, Tavaszi Sör ('Spring Beer'), Három Királyok ('Three Kings') and, under licence, Gold Fassl. Brau Union Hungária Breweries is largely owned by Brau AG of Austria, with breweries in Sopron, Martfu and Komárom. Brands include Soproni Ászok, Talléros, Arany Hordó ('Golden Barrel'), Sárkány Sör ('Dragon Beer') and, under licence, Amstel, Gösser, Heineken, Kaiser and Zlaty Bazant. Nagykanizsa Brewery produces beer under the brands of Kanizsai Világos, Kanizsai Kinizsi, Balatoni Világos and Paracelsus. A number of small and microbreweries have also emerged over the past few years.

Left: There is a wide variety of pubs and bars in central Budapest, reflecting the city's vibrant beer drinking culture. Some are styled like German or Austrian beerhalls; some feel like elegant turn-of-the-century restaurants; others have a modern, international flavour. This reflects the many and varied political and cultural forces which have influenced the city over the centuries.

Above: Dreher is a classic Hungarian brewery, which has been producing some of the most popular beers in the country since 1796. Based in Budapest, it is now owned by SABMiller.

STATISTICS

Total production: 4,676,000 hectolitres (198,129,000 gallons) per year
Consumption per capita: 73 litres (19 gallons) per year
Famous breweries: Brau Union Hungaria Sörgyarak; Borsodi; Dreher
Famous brands: Borsodi Bivaly; Dreher Classic; Soproni Ászok

Soproni Ászok

This light Hungarian bottled beer pours pale yellow and has a white head that quickly diminishes to leave light lacings on the glass. The aroma is light to moderate malt, with some hops, and the brew is slightly sweet, with a touch of bitterness.

The body of Soproni Ászok is watery and light, and softly carbonated. The finish is dry and discreet, but slightly bitter. The precursor of the modern Soproni Brewery, part of the Brau Union Hungaria Sörgyarak, was the Sopron Brewery and Malt Factory, which was founded in 1895. The brewery was badly damaged during World War II, and production did not restart until 1947. The malt-making function closed down in the 1960s. The name Ászok derives from the Hungarian name for the barrels or casks (called *ászok*) in which the beer is stored for secondary fermentation.

SPECIFICATIONS
Brewery: Brau Union Hungaria Sörgyarak
Location: Sopron
Style: Lager
Colour: Gold
Alcohol: 4.5%
Serving temperature: 8°C (46°F)
Food: Snacks, shellfish

Dreher Arany Ászok

One of the brews from the Dreher stable, this Hungarian lager is primarily a thirst-quencher. It pours pale yellow, with a small white head. It exudes a sweet, malty aroma with hints of corn and hops.

The flavour is sweet and malty, too, and there are also undertones of corn. There is plenty of carbonation, which produces a fizzy effect that might not be to everyone's taste, and the brew is light overall. It finishes quite well, with a pronounced bitter taste. All in all, this is quite a fair German-style lager. The company also produces a low-alcohol version, with an alcohol content of only 0.5%. Both brews have enjoyed considerable commercial success.

SPECIFICATIONS
Brewery: Dreher Sörgyar (SABMiller)
Location: Budapest
Style: Pilsener
Colour: Pale yellow
Alcohol: 4.7%
Serving temperature: 6°C (43°F)
Food: Pork, chicken, snacks

Dreher Classic

This is a very pure pilsener that pours a beautiful golden colour and has a small white head. The flavour is sweet and full of malt, with hints of hops and a discreet bitterness.

The aroma is slightly sour but far from unpleasant, hinting at malt, corn and spices. The Dreher company incorporates two breweries in Budapest and Nagykanizsa, as well as a centralized sales and distribution subsidiary registered in Budapest. Dreher brews beer following the greatest traditions in the Hungarian brewing industry coupled with world-class technology, which results in high-quality beer. The company's portfolio also includes premium beers made in Hungary under licence, such as the German Hofbrau and the Danish Tuborg, as well as famous imported beers such as Guinness and Kilkenny from Ireland.

SPECIFICATIONS
Brewery: Dreher Sörgyar
Location: Budapest
Style: Pilsener
Colour: Pale gold

Alcohol: 5.5%
Serving temperature: 8°C (46°F)
Food: Fish, savoury snacks

Borsodi Bivali

This is probably Hungary's strongest lager beer. It pours dark golden and has a thin white head. The aroma is slightly malty with some weak flavours of hops. Taste is full-bodied malty, though some metallic qualities follow.

The alcohol comes through strongly. Beer critics are enthusiastic about this brew, which they rate as one of the best beers produced in Hungary. (The word *bivaly*, incidentally, is Hungarian for 'buffalo'.) Borsodi is now a subsidiary of InBev, which specializes in strong beer brands. The company also produces Borsodi Sör, a traditional lager beer, which is brewed in the village of Bocs in northwestern Hungary. It also brews an alcohol-free beer, Borsodi Polo, which is a pale lager.

SPECIFICATIONS
Brewery: Borsodi Sörgyar (InBev)
Location: Budapest
Style: European strong lager

Colour: Rich gold
Alcohol: 6.5%
Serving temperature: 8°C (46°F)
Food: White meats, fish, snacks

Polish Beers

Although Poland is not famous for the range and style of its beers, it has a history of brewing stretching back into the Middle Ages. It was only in the nineteenth century, however, that brewing on a large scale became firmly established, and to acquire the necessary expertise the Polish breweries turned to Britain.

As well as ideas, the Polish industry imported brewing machinery and porter-style ales. Before that, Polish beer styles seemed to reflect the tastes of the different peoples who laid claim to Poland's territory at one time or another. Parts of Poland were annexed by Prussia, Russia and Austria in 1772; a small Polish state was left at the mercy of these three powers. In 1795, following a peasant insurrection, even that state was swallowed up, and many Poles fled the country. In 1807 Napoleon supported a renewed Polish state, but that was soon extinguished when the Russians defeated his army in 1812. A Russian-controlled Polish kingdom existed, but came to an end after a series of insurrections.

It is small wonder, then, that the Polish brewing industry had a chequered history. Even so, it continued to expand in the early years of the twentieth century. It was only during the economic crisis of the 1920s that growth slowed.

When Germany invaded in 1939 there were 137 Polish breweries, but World War II inflicted such devastation that virtually all of them were destroyed. It was at least a decade after 1945 before the industry was resurrected. Rather sadly, the sole survivor of Poland's native beers, Grodziskie, disappeared in the 1990s, deemed uneconomical by the master brewery, Lech.

Above: Warsaw is one of Europe's most cultured cities, but it was almost razed to the ground during World War II. The destruction took with it most of the city's breweries, and it was not until the 1950s that Warsaw's inhabitants began to enjoy widely available local brews once again.

STATISTICS

Total production: 29,200,000 hectolitres (771,382,300 gallons) per year
Consumption per capita: 75 litres (20 gallons) per year
Famous breweries: Bosman; Kompanie Piwowarska; Okocim; Warka; Tyskie; Zubr; Zywiec
Famous brands: Lech Premium; Okocim O.K.

Above: The Tyskie Brewery has an ancestry stretching back to the seventeenth century. As such it has come through numerous wars, and even the periodic extinction of Poland itself.

Bosman Full

A strong, mature lager with a full taste, this beer is best consumed quickly, before it has a chance to warm up. Golden in colour, Bosman Full has a foamy white head and a nose of malt and hops, along with a hint of caramel. The flavour is of sweet malts with a hoppy finish and aftertaste.

Bosman Full is one of two lagers brewed by the company, now owned by Carlsberg. The other is Bosman Special (6.6%). In terms of flavour there is not a great deal to choose between these respective lagers. Bosman, incidentally, is Polish for 'bosun', a reflection, perhaps, of Szczecin's (formerly Stettin's) long history as a seaport.

SPECIFICATIONS

Brewery: Bosman Browar Szczecin SA (Carlsberg)
Location: Szczecin
Style: Lager
Colour: Pale gold
Alcohol: 5.7%
Serving temperature: 6°–8°C (43°–46°F)
Food: Salad, bread and cheese

Kasztelan Jasne Pelne

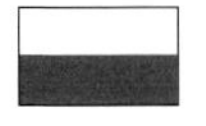

This is an attractive gold-coloured lager with an impressive creamy head. The aroma is light and dry, with a sweet malty undertone. The texture is clean, smooth and soft, the carbonation medium, and the finish quite sweet. Kasztelan is a good party lager, equally at home with light meals or as an aperitif.

The Kasztelan brewery is in the town of Sierpc, 125 km (80 miles) northwest of Warsaw. It produces around 615,000 hectolitres (16,000,000 gallons) of beer annually and is one of the leading breweries in the central region of the country. The company also owns a malting plant.

SPECIFICATIONS

Brewery: Kasztelan Browar
Location: Sierpc
Style: Lager
Colour: Dark gold
Alcohol: 6.2%
Serving temperature: 6°–8°C (43°–46°F)
Food: Cold meats, salads, or serve as an apéritif

Lech Premium

This beer has been described as the Polish equivalent of Heineken. Brewed in Poland since 1956, Lech Premium is a Pilsner-style beer that is pleasing to the eye, pouring a rich golden colour with a thick white head. Unlike some Pilsners, its flavour remains long after the bottle has been opened.

It has an aroma of corn and is good on the palate, with a mild flavour of hops. It does have an underlying and persistent sweetness, though, which may not be palatable to some drinkers. It is exceptionally smooth with a good malty flavour, but lacks bitterness. Some critics find it a little gassy and on the heavy side, but this is entirely a matter of opinion. Served as an apéritif, it is certainly effective in helping to work up an appetite.

SPECIFICATIONS
Brewery: Kompania Piwowarska
Location: Poznan
Style: Pilsner
Colour: Gold
Alcohol: 5.2%
Serving temperature: 6°–8°C (43°–46°F)
Food: Serve as an apéritif

Okocim O.K.

Okocim O.K. is a fine and delicate brew, deriving its quality from a recipe that incorporates the best of indigenous Polish hop varieties, luxurious barley and only the softest mountain water.

A refreshing drink, it is quite soft and impeccably balances the aromatics of hop and malt. The pure water of the Tatra mountain range is the most important ingredient in Okocim O.K., giving it a pure finish and making it universally enjoyable. The Okocim brewery reintroduced this handcrafted brew to celebrate the millennium, and the O.K. label remains mostly unchanged from its original design of 40 years ago. The beer itself helped to define 'Polish Pilsner style', in turn separating Polish beers from the many other European brands.

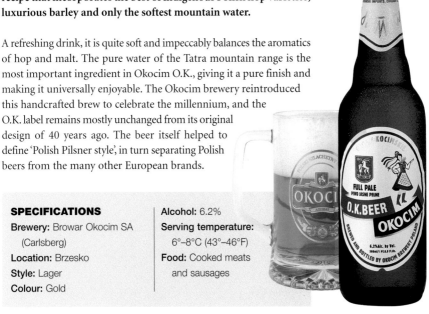

FULL PALE
PIWO JASNE PEŁNE
O.K.BEER
OKOCIM
BREWED AND BOTTLED BY OKOCIM BREWERY POLAND

SPECIFICATIONS
Brewery: Browar Okocim SA (Carlsberg)
Location: Brzesko
Style: Lager
Colour: Gold
Alcohol: 6.2%
Serving temperature: 6°–8°C (43°–46°F)
Food: Cooked meats and sausages

Tyskie Gronie

Gronie is the latest in a long line of beers brewed in the Polish town of Tychy, where the brewing industry was first established in the seventeenth century. The beer pours a pale golden colour, with a thick white head that lingers for a considerable time.

The aroma is reminiscent of hay. At first sight it may seem little different from any other eastern European style of lager beer, but this is not the case. The flavour is distinctive, with a nice unexpected hoppy richness at the end. First reports about the brewery come from 1613, when the Promnice family owned it. At the end of the nineteenth century the Tyskie brewery was among the biggest and most modern breweries in Europe, a position it maintains to this day.

SPECIFICATIONS
Brewery: Tyskie Browary Ksiazece (KP-SABMiller)
Location: Tychy
Style: Pilsner
Colour: Pale gold
Alcohol: 5.6%
Serving temperature: 8°C (46°F)
Food: Chicken or seafood salads, or as a simple apéritif

Warka Strong

This lager pours a beautiful, dark golden-honey colour of a deep lustre and has a creamy head. It has the transparency of springwater, as well as an excellent body and taste. The aroma is sweet and grainy, with a strong undercurrent of alcohol. It is very well saturated with carbon dioxide.

Warka Strong tastes of peppery, sweet malt and has herbal hop bitterness that becomes slightly metallic in the finish. A satisfying drink, this lager might be slightly too sweet for some palates. The Warka brewing tradition dates all the way back to the fifteenth century, when in 1478 Warka brewers received the exclusive privilege to supply the royal court at Warsaw.

SPECIFICATIONS
Brewery: Browary Warka (Heineken)
Location: Warka
Style: Lager
Colour: Dark gold
Alcohol: 7.0%
Serving temperature: 8°C (46°F)
Food: Drink as an apéritif, or serve with a crisp salad

Zubr Jasne Pelne

Jasne Pelne is usually translated as 'full light beer'. It means a pale lager of full strength, at least 10° plato (a measure of specific density relating to the amount of malt used when brewing).

Most Polish beers fall into this category. It covers beers in the Pilsner style and in the Export or Spezial (Specjal) styles. Those at the weaker end are like a Czech pale lager – a sort of session-strength Pils. Zubr lager, brewed in Bialystok in eastern Poland, is named after the bison which still roam the nearby Bialowieza forest. This typical lager has an off-white head. The flavour is sweet and malty, with some notes of grain and herbs. The body is rather thin, and there is a slight bitterness in the finish.

SPECIFICATIONS
Brewery: Pivo Dojlidy Zubr
Location: Bialystok
Style: Lager
Colour: Golden
Alcohol: 5.5%
Serving temperature: 6°–8°C (43°–46°F)
Food: Serve as an aperitif

Zywiec Jasne Pelne

Zywiec's Jasne Pelne is a good 'middle of the road' lager with a medium head that quickly dissipates. The initial aroma is of malt and honey, and there is a bewildering array of flavours including sweet, salt, sour and bitter.

The alcohol is perhaps a little too quick to separate itself in the mouth, causing the full-bodied palate to seem a bit strong. It is quite refreshing and soft, with a slight sweetness and little bitterness. In summary, it is a fairly typical mass-produced lager. Now owned by Heineken, the Zywiec Brewery belonged to the Habsburg family until the beginning of World War II. It produces a range of beers in embossed cans, as well as bottled varieties.

SPECIFICATIONS
Brewery: Browar Zywiec (Heineken)
Location: Zywiec
Style: Lager
Colour: Gold
Alcohol: 5.6%
Serving temperature: 6°–8°C (43°–46°F)
Food: Chicken, lamb cutlets, fish

Asian Beers

The most significant markets for beer in the Far East are Japan and China, both of which rank among the world's leading beer consumers, even though neither country has a real beer brewing tradition. Beer was introduced to China by the Germans and Russians at the start of the twentieth century.

The number of breweries in China is now approaching the 1000 mark, with businesses ranging from small local breweries to giant state-owned industries. Japan, however, is the largest per capita beer consumer in the Far East. Beer arrived in Japan around 50 years earlier than in China, and Kirin, the country's first commercial brewery, was established in 1870 by an American. The first Japanese-owned brewery was launched in 1876. After rapid growth in the 1890s, there was a major consolidation of breweries in 1906. Introduction of beer tax laws in 1908, which enforced a minimum production level of 180,000 litres per year, meant that smaller breweries could not survive, concentrating the industry into the hands of a few companies. A sudden growth in microbreweries and brewpubs came with the repeal of these laws in 1994.

Brewing traditions vary widely across the rest of Asia, although as a rule beer consumption is relatively low compared to most of Europe. India still feels the legacy of English colonial influence in its preference for rich, dark stouts and India pale ale, but most beer drunk in India is imported. One of the largest brewers in Southeast Asia is San Miguel of the Philippines, which has production facilities across the region. It is also one of the oldest, having been established for more than 100 years.

Left: Asia is noted for the fine quality of its pale lagers. Export sales of bottled and canned beers to the United States, South America and Europe have grown rapidly over the past 20 years. China is the world's largest beer producer in terms of pure volume.

Above: A poster for the Japanese Asahi beer. Asahi is a perfect example of a regional Asian beer capturing real export success in today's global marketplace.

STATISTICS

Total production: 396,638,000 hectolitres (10,478,067,000 gallons) per year

Consumption per capita: 10 litres (3 gallons) per year

Famous breweries: Asahi; Asia Pacific Breweries; Boon Rawd Brewery Company Ltd; Cambrew Limited; Chunghua Beer Company Ltd; Kirin; PT Multi Bintang Indonesia

Famous brands: Angkor; Asahi; Bir Bintang Pilsener; Kingfisher; Kirin Beer; Sapporo; Tiger; Tsingtao

Kingfisher

Kingfisher is a very popular lager, although not to everyone's taste. It pours with a wispy little head and a tiny bit of lace.

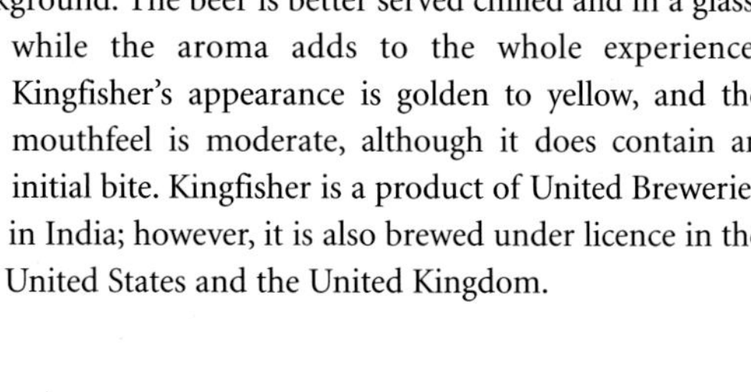

The aroma is a pleasant mix of cereal grains and a faint yeast background. The beer is better served chilled and in a glass, while the aroma adds to the whole experience. Kingfisher's appearance is golden to yellow, and the mouthfeel is moderate, although it does contain an initial bite. Kingfisher is a product of United Breweries in India; however, it is also brewed under licence in the United States and the United Kingdom.

SPECIFICATIONS
Brewery: United Breweries
Location: Bangalore, Karnataka, India
Style: Adjunct lager
Colour: Pale yellow
Alcohol: Not listed
Serving temperature: Chilled
Food: Curries, especially coconut-based

Bengal Tiger

A rather sugary-sweet lager, Bengal Tiger is nevertheless becoming an increasingly popular choice in Indian restaurants in Europe.

Straw gold in colour, it has a light malt aroma. The bottled lager is produced by Mysore Breweries of Bangalore. In common with other Indian bottled lagers, Bengal Tiger should be served chilled, and drunk with spicy oriental food to be appreciated fully. Many drinkers consider it to be too bland for their palates.

SPECIFICATIONS
Brewery: Mysore Breweries
Location: Mysore, Karnataka, India
Style: Adjunct lager
Colour: Straw gold
Alcohol: 5%
Serving temperature: Chilled
Food: Curries, especially coconut-based

Chunghua Zhong Hua

The Chunghua beer company, like Tsingtao in Shandong province, was originally founded by German settlers, this time in the coastal province of Zhejiang in eastern China. The area was subject to German colonial rule until the early twentieth century, in much the same way that Hong Kong was under British rule.

Today both the region and the brewery are under Chinese ownership. Although less well known outside China than Tsingtao, Zhong Hua beer is nonetheless one of the country's leading exported beers. It is mainly available in areas with large Chinese communities, and you will often find this beer served in Chinese restaurants. Zhong Hua is a straightforward, light, easy-drinking pale golden lager with a modest hop profile.

SPECIFICATIONS
Brewery: Chunghua Beer Company Ltd
Location: Chunghua, Zhejiang Province, China
Style: Lager
Colour: Pale blonde
Alcohol: 5%
Serving temperature: 8°C (46.4°F)
Food: Simple vegetable and rice-based dishes

Tsingtao

Founded in 1903 by German settlers in the port of Tsingtao (now Qingdao), Tsingtao (pronounced 'ching-dow') was one of the first commercial breweries in China and is currently one of its largest.

Its flagship golden lager is the best-selling beer in China and by far the best known Chinese beer worldwide, having first been introduced to the United States in 1972 and today accounting for around 80% of Chinese beer exports. Produced using spring water from the Laoshan mountains, and malt and yeast imported from Canada and Australia, Tsingtao has a light hoppy aroma and a well-balanced flavour.

SPECIFICATIONS
Brewery: Tsingtao
Location: Qingdao, Shandong Province, China
Style: Lager
Colour: Pale yellow
Alcohol: 4.8%
Serving temperature: 8°C (46.4°F)
Food: Steamed or poached fish

Bir Bintang Pilsener

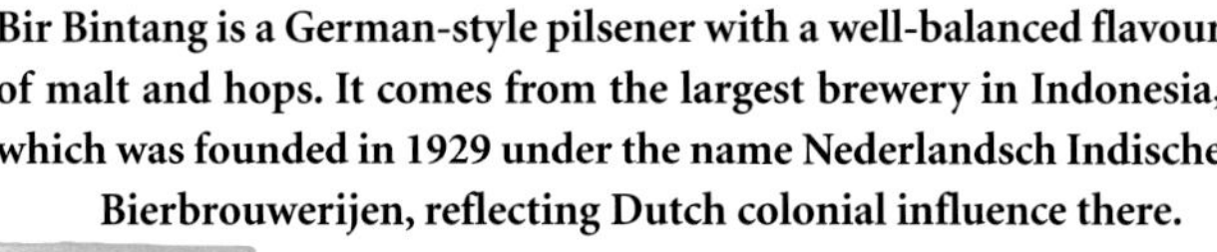

Bir Bintang is a German-style pilsener with a well-balanced flavour of malt and hops. It comes from the largest brewery in Indonesia, which was founded in 1929 under the name Nederlandsch Indische Bierbrouwerijen, reflecting Dutch colonial influence there.

The company was taken over by Heineken in 1936 and started brewing Heineken beer. Heineken withdrew from the region in 1957, however, and prohibited the use of its brand name. As a result, the beer was renamed Perusahaan Bir Bintang. When Heineken resumed brewing in Indonesia in 1967, the beer was relaunched as Bintang Baru. It has been known as Bir Bintang since 2002. The brewery also produces Guinness under licence.

SPECIFICATIONS
Brewery: PT Multi Bintang Indonesia
Location: Surabaya, Indonesia
Style: Pilsener
Colour: Golden yellow
Alcohol: 4.8%
Serving temperature: 8°C (46.4°F)
Food: Goes well with spicy Indonesian food

Boon Rawd Singha

The first and still the largest brewery in Thailand, Boon Rawd was founded in 1933 by Phraya Bhirom Bhakdi, using German technology to produce pilsener-style beers.

Today, Boon Rawd is a diverse company with product lines including bottled water, tea and coffee, as well as its three beer brands, Singha, Leo and Thai Beer. Singha is a full-bodied all-malt lager with a prominent herbal hop character. Also available is Singha Gold Light, a low-calorie and low-alcohol version of Singha with a light, refreshing flavour. Leo is a standard light, golden lager, while Thai Beer is a slightly stronger beer.

SPECIFICATIONS
Brewery: Rawd Brewery Company Ltd
Location: Bangkok, Thailand
Style: Lager
Colour: Golden yellow
Alcohol: 6%
Serving temperature: 6°–8°C
Food: Fish and seafood

Tiger Beer

Tiger Beer is the best-selling beer in Singapore, an all-malt golden lager brewed with malt imported from Europe and Australia, and hops imported from Germany.

The yeast strain is also European, developed exclusively for the brewery in the Netherlands by Heineken. It is the leading brand of Asia Pacific Breweries, founded in 1931 under the name Malayan Breweries Limited as a joint venture between Heineken and Fraser & Neave. Although the brewery uses imported ingredients, all its beers are brewed exclusively at the two plants in Singapore and Kuala Lumpur, Malaysia, unlike many other Asian beers which are brewed under licence in Europe and the United States. It is one of the best-known Asian beers in the west, largely thanks to its popularity with Allied troops stationed in the Far East during World War II.

SPECIFICATIONS
Brewery: Asia Pacific Breweries
Location: Alexandria Point, Singapore
Style: Lager
Colour: Pale straw yellow
Alcohol: 5%
Serving temperature: 6°–8°C (42.8°–46.4°F)
Food: Spicy oriental dishes

Angkor Beer

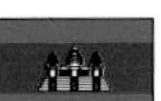

Most beers drunk in Cambodia are imported brands such as Tiger, San Miguel and Heineken, but the country has its own national beer, Angkor, produced in the port city of Sihanoukville by Cambrew, which was founded in 1990.

It is named after the majestic Angkor Wat temple, which is depicted on the labels on the bottle and was built by the Khmer empire which ruled in the ninth and tenth centuries AD. The beer is a typically European-style golden lager with a full body, a soft bitterness and a light, hoppy aroma. Angkor beer has enjoyed a steadily growing popularity overseas in recent years, and is becoming a more common sight in the bars and specialist drink shops of Europe and the United States, with major export markets in Japan and Canada. It comes in a variety of formats: bottled, canned and draught.

SPECIFICATIONS
Brewery: Cambrew Limited
Location: Sihanoukville, Cambodia
Style: Lager
Colour: Golden yellow
Alcohol: 5.2%
Serving temperature: 6°–8°C (42.8°–46.4°F)
Food: Amocfish (fish soup with coconut milk)

Asahi Super Dry

Japan's leading brewery was founded in 1889 as the Osaka brewery, and launched the first Asahi beer in 1892. In 1906, Asahi merged with two other breweries – Japan Beer Brewery Ltd and Sapporo Beer Company – to form the Dai Nippon Breweries Company.

In 1949, Dai Nippon was forced to separate into two companies, of which Asahi was the smaller. It remained that way until the late 1980s, when it launched Asahi Super Dry. The beer's huge success, both in Japan and around the world, saw the company rocket in size. Asahi Super Dry has a smooth, light flavour, achieved through a longer maturation period. In this respect, it is similar to a classic German pilsener, but with a much lighter hop profile. The result is an astringently dry beer with a delicate flavour. Asahi also brews Asahi Draft Beer Fujisan and Asahi Super Malt.

SPECIFICATIONS

Brewery: Asahi
Location: Tokyo, Japan
Style: Lager
Colour: Golden yellow
Alcohol: 5%
Serving temperature: 6°–7°C (42.8°–44.6°F)
Food: Traditional Japanese cuisine, especially sushi

Kirin Beer

Kirin Beer is a crisp, golden pilsener-style lager flavoured with Saaz and Hallertau hops for a refreshing floral bitterness. It is matured in cold cellars for up to two months to give it a smoother, lighter body and a richer, fuller flavour.

In Japan it is bottled unpasteurized and unfiltered, but when exported it tends to be sold in a filtered form. Kirin beers are also brewed under licence in the United States and Europe. The brewery, originally known as Spring Valley, was founded in Yokohama in 1869 and can claim to have been one of Japan's earliest commercial breweries. While Kirin Beer has been the best-selling beer brand in Japan continuously since 1888, Kirin became the country's leading brewer only in 1954, a position it has held ever since.

SPECIFICATIONS

Brewery: Kirin
Location: Tokyo, Japan
Style: Pilsener
Colour: Golden yellow
Alcohol: 4.9%
Serving temperature: 8°C (46.4°F)
Food: Sushi, sashimi and tempura

Hitachino Nest Red Rice Beer

This distinctive beer has a grainy malt aroma with subtle floral hop notes and an underlying yeasty fruitiness, with notes of cherries, oranges, pears and apples.

The slightly hazy orangey colour comes not from the malts used, as you might expect, but from the use of red rice, which also gives the beer a crisp, clean, refreshing character with a slightly sweet edge, similar to a saké. There is also a delicate hint of bitter, citrussy hops in the flavour. The high alcohol content gives it a spicy, mouth-drying tang and a pleasant warmth in the finish. The use of rice reflects the brewery's 1823 origins as a saké brewer.

SPECIFICATIONS

Brewery: Kiuchi Brewery
Location: Naka-gun, Ibaragi, Japan
Style: Belgian abbey double
Colour: Dark amber-orange
Alcohol: 8.5%
Serving temperature: 8°–10°C (46.4°–50°F)
Food: Yakitori-style grilled chicken

Sapporo Silver Sapporo

In Japan, the flagship beer of the Sapporo brewery is usually sold in bottles and is known as Sapporo Black Label, after its distinctive black label that bears the brewery's silver star emblem.

Elsewhere, the bottled beer is known as Sapporo Premium, but it also comes in stylish silver cans as either Silver Sapporo or Sapporo Draft. It is a light, refreshing golden lager with a soft, malty aroma and a gently bitter hop flavour. It was launched in Japan in 1977, but the Sapporo brewery has a history that stretches back to 1876, when Seibei Nakagawa was employed by the Japanese government to oversee construction of a brewery in Hokkaido.

SPECIFICATIONS

Brewery: Sapporo Breweries Ltd
Location: Hokkaido, Japan
Style: Lager
Colour: Golden yellow
Alcohol: 4.5%
Serving temperature: 6°–8°C (42.8°–46.4°F)
Food: Light pasta or rice

ER'S LAGER
F
RALIA'S CLASSIC
ER SINCE 1888
355mL
FOSTER'S®
CARLTON & UNITED BREWERIES LTD
77 SOUTHBANK BOULEVARD SOUTHBANK VIC 3006
BEER · PRODUCT OF AUSTRALIA

Australian and New Zealand Beers

Brewing in Australia and New Zealand started with the arrival of European settlers in the late eighteenth century – the first record of brewing in Australia dates from 1794, when John Boston produced a beer using maize imported from India (instead of barley) and the stems and leaves of cape gooseberries as a bittering agent.

Aside from the difficulty of obtaining ingredients, early brewers in Australia also had to deal with an unfavourable climate. The effect of the heat on the top-fermenting yeast (used to produce English-style ales) meant that brewing was an unpredictable business at best, and even when attempts were successful the beer would not keep for very long.

By the late nineteenth century, the introduction of refrigeration by brewing pioneers such as the Foster brothers meant that ales had been mostly replaced by bottom-fermenting golden lagers, which remain the most popular style. Meanwhile, in New Zealand, where the climate was similar to that of northern Europe, ales could be brewed successfully and remained popular in this country even after the introduction of lagers.

The domestic market in Australia is dominated by two giant companies, Carlton and United Breweries (a division of the international Foster's Brewing Group) and New Zealand's Lion Nathan. Beer is still hugely popular, although since the early 1980s it has been in steady decline due to the increasing popularity of wine. Brewing in New Zealand, by contrast, has historically been severely affected by the influence of the temperance movement. Lion Nathan had its beginnings in 1923, for instance, when 10 of the country's largest breweries merged in order to survive.

Left: Foster's lager is undoubtedly one of the world's best-known beer brands, a brand which is backed by a strikingly efficient advertising campaign. Alongside Castlemaine XXXX, Foster's has given Australia a worldwide presence on the beer markets, but New Zealand is also claiming an increased market share through quality premium beers such as Steinlager (produced under the giant Lion Nathan Group).

Above: Part of the reason for the major success of Australian beers in export is the Australian identity itself.

STATISTICS

Total production: 20,300,000 hectolitres (536,270,000 gallons) per year

Consumption per capita: 82 litres (22 gallons) per year

Famous breweries: Castlemaine Perkins; Foster's Brewing Group Ltd; Lion Breweries; Malt Shovel; Swan Brewery

Famous brands: Castelmaine XXXX; Foster's; James Squire Original Amber Ale; Steinlager; Swan Draught

James Boag's Premium Lager

James Boag's Premium Lager is a European-style lager brewed from the finest quality pilsener malts. This beer is fermented at a lower temperature than most Australian lagers and employs an extended maturation period. These combine with a mixture of kettle and late hopping to yield a crisp, pale lager that provide an excellent accompaniment to fine food.

Originally called the Esk Brewery, James Boag's business was established on the banks of the Esk River in Launceston in 1881. When James Boag I and his son, James Boag II, took over the brewery, the name Esk was retained, although it was frequently referred to thereafter as Boag's Brewery. Under the direction of James Boag and his son, the brewery quickly established a reputation for brewing the highest quality beers.

SPECIFICATIONS
Brewery: James Boag and Son
Location: Launceston, Tasmania
Style: Lager
Colour: Golden
Alcohol: 5%
Serving temperature: 5°–7°C (41°–45°F)
Food: Spicy dishes; fried fish and seafood

Victoria Bitter

Australia's most popular full-strength beer, Victoria Bitter, or VB as it is generally known, was launched in the 1890s and has a tradition of rewarding hard work and hard play.

Over the last ten years it has been a consistent winner in the esteemed Australian Liquor Industry Awards (ALIA), more recently picking up 'Best Full Strength Beer' in 2001, 'Tap Beer of the Year' in 2002 and 'Best Full Strength Beer' again in 2003. VB is a full-flavoured brew, less malty in character and slightly darker than CUB's traditional lagers. A gentle fruitiness in the aroma complements the sweet malt on the mid-palate balancing perfectly with a robust, hop bitterness.

SPECIFICATIONS
Brewery: Carlton and United Breweries
Location: Melbourne, Victoria
Style: Full Strength Bitter Lager
Colour: Golden
Alcohol: 4.9%
Serving temperature: 8°–10°C (46°–50°F)
Food: Pizza, chicken

Castlemaine XXXX

This is a pale malty lager brewed with whole hops for a refreshing bitter flavour. Castlemaine Brewery was founded in Castlemaine, Victoria, in 1859 by brothers Nicholas and Edwin Fitzgerald.

XXXX
CASTLEMAINE
XXXX
EXPORT LAGER
CASTLEMAINE PERKINS
BRISBANE • AUSTRALIA

In 1877 they took over an ailing distillery in the Brisbane suburb of Milton, where they started brewing Castlemaine XXX Sparkling Ale. This was joined by XXXX Sparkling Ale in 1894, but the Queensland heat caused problems in the brewing process. In 1920, an Austrian brewer by the name of Alois Wilhelm Leitner, was called in, and he developed a lighter bottom-fermented recipe that was launched as XXXX Bitter Ale. Castlemaine later merged with Perkins Brewery of Brisbane and in 1992 became part of New Zealand's Lion Nathan group.

SPECIFICATIONS
Brewery: Castlemaine Perkins
Location: Brisbane, Queensland
Style: Lager
Colour: Pale golden yellow
Alcohol: 4.8%
Serving temperature: 6°–8°C (42.8°–46.4°F)
Food: Spicy food such as Thai curries

Foster's Lager

Australia's original lager has a smooth texture and a well-rounded malty flavour on the palate, with a light hop presence in the finish. It was originally brewed in 1887 in Melbourne by two brothers from New York.

IMPORTED
FOSTER'S LAGER
FOSTER'S
FOSTER'S
AUSTRALIA'S FAMOUS BEER

Although the brewery still bears their name, their involvement with the company ended after just 18 months, when they returned to their native New York. Before they left, however, they introduced an innovative refrigeration process that enabled the brewing of lighter European-style golden lagers in the harsh Australian climate. Fosters is now Australia's best-known beer brand internationally, and it is available in more than 150 countries worldwide. This highly successful brand recognition is largely the result of a phase of massive international expansion which took place throughout the 1980s.

SPECIFICATIONS
Brewery: Foster's Brewing Group Ltd
Location: Melbourne, Australia
Style: Lager
Colour: Pale golden yellow
Alcohol: 4.9%
Serving temperature: 5°–7°C (41°–44.6°F)
Food: Salads, shellfish

James Squire Original Amber Ale

The original Malt Shovel brewery was founded in 1795 by James Squire, a brewer, publican and convicted highway robber who was deported to Australia.

The James Squire Original Amber Ale available today is an imitation of the English-style pale ales that were brewed by the first Malt Shovel brewery. It is brewed with a blend of crystal and caramel malts to give it a distinctive coppery colour and a rich, sweet, nutty malt flavour, while late hopping with Willamette hops from Tasmania provides a refreshingly bitter citrussy grapefruit finish. The brewery also produces a heavily hopped pilsener with a fragrant herby, floral aroma balanced by a mellow malt flavour.

SPECIFICATIONS
Brewery: Malt Shovel
Location: Sydney, New South Wales
Style: English pale ale
Colour: Copper red
Alcohol: 5%
Serving temperature: 10°C (50°F)
Food: Lamb, beef or game dishes

Swan Draught

The first commercial brewery in Perth, founded in 1837, was called Albion. The original Swan brewery came later, in 1857, formed by Frederick Sherwood, who settled in the area which is today known as Sherwood Court.

The brewery was leased to Captain John Ferguson and William Mumme, whose expertise in German beer styles greatly enhanced the quality of Swan beers. It later came under the sole ownership of Mumme, who in 1928 also acquired ownership of Albion, which by then was known as Emu. Today the Swan brewery is part of the huge Lion Nathan Group of drinks producers. Swan Draught is its flagship brand and the leading lager in Western Australia. It is a smooth, easy-drinking beer with a malty flavour balanced by a gentle bitterness provided by Tasmanian hops.

SPECIFICATIONS
Brewery: Swan Brewery
Location: Perth, Western Australia
Style: Lager
Colour: Golden yellow
Alcohol: 4.8%
Serving temperature: 6°–8°C (42.8°–46.4°F)
Food: Barbecued sausages

Tui

Tui is an India Pale Ale-style beer from New Zealand. Although it claims to be brewed in the IPA style, Tui is in fact a brown lager with little hop aroma or bitterness.

Tui East India Pale Ale originated from the Tui Brewery in Mangatainoka in the Wairarapa region of North Island New Zealand. The product is now a brand owned and brewed by Dominion Breweries. Henry Wagstaff opened the Tui brewery at Mangatainoka in 1889, attracted by the water of the Mangatainoka River. In 1903 he sold it to Henry Cowan, who developed the prize-winning East India Pale Ale. As the factory expanded, a seven-storey brew tower was built in 1931, so brewers could use gravity to turn malt into beer. Which was fine, except that the builders forgot to put in a lift and stairs, a problem later rectified.

SPECIFICATIONS
Brewery: Dominion Breweries
Location: Mangatainoka
Style: Dark lager
Colour: Honey
Alcohol: 4%
Serving temperature: 8°–10°C (46°–50°F)
Food: Barbecued meats

Lion Steinlager

Steinlager is the pilsener-style lager made by Lion Breweries. It has a distinctive grassy aroma and clean, crisp hop bitterness on the palate leading to a dry, astringent finish.

Lion was formed in 1923, when many of New Zealand's leading breweries merged in a bid to fight off prohibitive legislation. The new company was called New Zealand Breweries, but was renamed Lion after one of its strongest brands in 1977. Prior to the merger, Lion beers had been brewed by the Great Northern Brewery, which had been founded in 1860. Lion Breweries is a division of the Lion Nathan Group, which is a major producer of wines and beers throughout New Zealand and Australia. Steinlager is brewed in Newmarket, a suburb of Auckland, on New Zealand's North Island.

SPECIFICATIONS
Brewery: Lion Breweries
Location: Auckland
Style: Pilsener
Colour: Pale golden yellow
Alcohol: 5%
Serving temperature: 6°–8°C (43°–46°F)
Food: An appetising aperitif

Index

Picture Credits

All pictures © Istituto Geographico DeAgostini Italy, with the exception of:

6: Corbis (Owen Franken), 8: Molson Breweries, 9: Corbis (Cathrine Wessel), 10(t): Oland Brewer/Interbrew, 10(b): Amsterdam Brewing Company, 11(t): Creemore Springs, 12(all): McAuslan Brewing, 13(all): Molson Breweries, 14(t): Moosehead Breweries, 14(b): Amber Books, 15(b): Amber Books, 16: Corbis (Dave Bartruff, Inc.), 17: Bridgeport Brewing Company, 18(t): Anchor Brewing Co, 18(b): Anheuser-Busch, 19(t): Anheuser-Busch, 20(t): Bridgeport Brewing Company: 20(b): Brooklyn Brewery, 21(t): Coors Brewing Company, 21(b): Goose Island Beer Company, 22(t): Great Lakes Brewing Company, 22(b): Latrobe Brewing, 23(t): Amber Books, 24(t): Amber Books, 24(b): Old Dominion Brewing Company, 25(t): Pabst Brewing Company, 25(b): Pensylvania Brewing Company, 26(t): Pike Pub & Brewery, 26(b): Redhook Ale Brewery, 27(t): Rogue Ales, 28(t): Miller Brewing Co., 28(b): Sierra Nevada Brewing Co., 29(t): Stone Brewing Company, 29(b): D.G. Yuengling & Son, Inc., 30: Corbis (Steve Raymer), 31: Corbis (Carl & Ann Purcell), 33(t): Especialidad Cerveceras, 36: Corbis (Annebicque Bernard), 37: Corbis (Bob Krist), 38(b): Egils Skallagrimsson Brewery, 37(all): Viking Brewery, 40: Heritage Image Partnership, 41: Hansa Bryggeri, 42(all): Aass Bryggeri, 43(t): Hansa Bryggeri, 43(b): Carlsberg, 44: Getty Images (Ted Wood), 45: (Jämtlands Bryggeri), 46(t): Carlsberg, 46(b): Jämtlands Bryggeri, 47(t): Jämtlands Bryggeri, 47(b): Slottskällans Bryggeri, 48: Sinebrychoff, 49: Heritage Image Partnership, 50(t): Finlandia Sahti Oy, 50(b): Hartwall (S&N), 51(t): Lammin Sahti Oy, 51(b): Sinebrychoff, 52: Corbis (Steve Raymer), 53: Getty Images (Carl Mydans), 54(t): Albani Bryggerierne AS, 54(b): Brøckhouse, 55(t): Carlsberg, 56(b): Amber Books, 58: Corbis (Michael St. Maur Sheil), 59: Corbis (Marvin Koner), 61(t): Diageo, 62: Corbis (Todd Gipstein), 63: Corbis (Bo Zaunders), 64(t): Belhaven Brewign Company, 65(b): Tennent Caledonian Breweries, 66: Corbis (Bruce Burkhardt), 67: Corbis (Kim Sayer), 68(b): Black Sheep Brewery Plc, 69(t): Amber Books, 69(b): Fuller, Smith & Turner Plc, 70(b): Amber Books, 71(t): Amber Books, 72(b): Samuel Smith's, 73(t): Amber Books, 73(b): T&R Theakston Ltd., 74: Corbis (Paul Seheult; Eye Ubiquitous), 75: Corbis (Owen Franken), 78: Corbis (Rougemont Maurice), 79: Corbis (Leonard de Selva), 82(t): Brasseries Kronenbourg (S&N), 83(t): Brasseries Kronenbourg (S&N), 83(b): Private Collection, 84: Getty Images (Richard Elliott), 85: Brasserie Simon, 86(t): Brasserie Bofferding, 87(b): Brasserie Simon, 88: Corbis (Bob Krist), 89: Corbis (Dave Bartruff), 91(b): InBev, 92(t): NV Brouwerijen Alken-Maes, 95(b): InBev, 100: Corbis (Annebicque Bernard), 101: Corbis (Floris Leeuwenberg), 102(all): Bavaria Brouwerij NV, 103(t): Amber Books, 104(b): Grolsche Bierbrouwerij NV, 106(b): InBev, 107(t): InBev, 108: Getty Images (Art Wolfe), 109: Corbis (Barnabas Bosshart), 110(t): Tramdepot Brauerei, 110(b): BFM Brasserie des Franches-Montagnes, 111(t): Brauerei Eichhof, 112: Corbis (Jan Nienheysen), 113: Corbis (Wolfgang Kaehler), 116(t): Berliner Kindl Brauerei, 117(t): Binding Brauerei, 118(b): DAB, 120(t): Brauerei P.J. Fruh, 121(b): Friesisches Bauhaus, 124(all): Franziskaner Bräu, 126: Corbis (Richard Klune), 127: Corbis (Jack Hollingsworth), 132: Corbis (Annebicque Bernard), 133: Corbis (Bob Krist), 134(t): Schloss Eggenberg, 135(t): Brau Union Osterreich AG, 135(b): Ottakringer Brauerei Harmer AG, 136(t): Brau Union Osterreich AG, 136(b): Stieglbrauerei zu Salzburg, 137(t): Brauerei Schwechat, 137(b): Brau Union Osterreich AG, 138: Corbis (Dave G. Houser), 139: Corbis (Petr Josek), 140(t): Budweiser Budvar, NC, 140(b): Amber Books, 141(t): Amber Books, 141(b): SABMiller, 142: Getty Images (Wilfried Krecichwost), 143: SABMiller, 144(t): Heineken International, 144(b): Amber Books, 145(all): Amber Books, 146: Getty Images (Walter Bibikow), 147: SABMiller, 148(t): Brau Union Hungaria, 148(b): SABMiller, 149(t) SABMiller, 149(b): InBev, 150: Getty Images (Janicek), 151: SABMiller, 152(all): Amber Books, 153(t): SABMiller, 153(b): Carlsberg-Okocim SA, 154(t): SABMiller, 154(b): Heineken International, 155(t): SABMiller, 155(b): Heineken International, 156: Corbis (Robert Maass), 157: Corbis (Swim Ink 2, LLC), 158(t): United Breweries, 158(b): Amber Books, 160(all): Amber Books, 161(t): Asia Pacific Breweries, 161(b): Cambrew Limited, 163(t): Kuchi Brewery, 163(b): Sapporo Breweries, 164: Corbis (Will Burgess), 165: Corbis (O. Alamany & E. Vicens), 166(t): J. Boag & Son Brewing Ltd, 166(b): Scottish & Newcastle, 168(b): Swan Brewery, 169(t): DB Breweries